for 11 - 14s

BOOK 4

CHRISTIAN FOCUS PUBLICATIONS

We believe that the Bible is God's word to mankind, and that it contains everything we need to know in order to be reconciled with God and live in a way that is pleasing to him. Therefore, we believe it is vital to teach young teens accurately from the Bible, being careful to teach each passage's true meaning in an appropriate way for the age group, rather than selecting a 'teen's message' from a Biblical passage.

© TⁿT Ministries
29 Buxton Gardens, Acton, London, W3 9LE
Tel: +44 (0)20 8992 0450 Fax: +44 (0)20 8896 1847
e-mail: sales@tntministries.org.uk

Published in 2002 by Christian Focus Publications Ltd.
Geanies House, Fearn, Tain, Ross-shire, IV20 1TW
Tel: +44 (0)1862 871 011 Fax: +44 (0)1862 871 699
e-mail: **info@christianfocus.com**
www.christianfocus.com

The puzzles have been prepared using the New International Version of the Bible.
Cover design by Profile Design

This book and others in the series can be purchased from your local Christian bookshop. Alternatively you can write to TⁿT Ministries direct or place your order with the publisher.

ISBN 1-85792-707-9

TⁿT Ministries (which stands for Teaching and Training Ministries) was launched in February 1993 by Christians from a broad variety of denominational backgrounds who were concerned that teaching the Bible to children be taken seriously. The leaders were in charge of the Sunday School of 50 teachers at St Helen's Bishopsgate, an evangelical church in the City of London, for 13 years, during which time a range of Biblical teaching materials was developed. TⁿT Ministries also runs training days for Sunday School teachers.

CONTENTS

On the Way for 11-14s / Book 4

Contributors

Preparation of Bible material:
Wendy Barber
Thalia Blundell
Rachel Garforth-Bles

Editing:
David Jackman

Activities & Puzzles:
Wendy Barber
Thalia Blundell
Jennefer Lord
Nick Margesson

On The Way for 11-14s works on a 3 year syllabus consisting of 6 books. It builds on the 9-11s syllabus and introduces young teens to study the Bible in a way which is challenging and intellectually stretching. Because they are often unprepared to take things at face value and are encouraged to question everything, it is important to satisfy the mind while touching the heart. Therefore, some of the lessons are designed to introduce the idea of further Bible study skills, e.g. the use of a concordance, a character study, studying a single verse or a passage.

Lessons are grouped in series, each of which is introduced by a series overview stating the aims of the series, the lesson aim for each week, and an appropriate memory verse. Every lesson, in addition to an aim, has study notes to enable the teacher to understand the Bible passage, a suggestion to focus attention on the study to follow, a 'Question Section' and an activity for the group to do. The Question Section consists of 2-3 questions designed to help in discussing the application of the Bible passage. The course can be joined at any time during its 3 year cycle.

To prepare a Bible lesson properly takes at least one evening (2-3 hours). It is helpful to read the Bible passage several days before teaching it to allow time to mull over what it is saying.

When preparing a lesson the following steps should be taken -

1. PRAY!

In a busy world this is very easy to forget. We are unable to understand God's word without his help and we need to remind ourselves of that fact before we start.

2. READ THE BIBLE PASSAGE

This should be done *before* reading the lesson manual. Our resource is the Bible, not what someone says about it. The Bible study notes in the lesson manual are a commentary on the passage to help you understand it.

3. LOOK AT THE LESSON AIM

This should reflect the main teaching of the passage. Plan how that can be packaged appropriately for the age group you teach.

4. TEACHING THE BIBLE PASSAGE

This should take place in the context of simple Bible study. Do ensure that the children use the same version of the Bible. Prior to the lesson decide how the passage will be read, (e.g. one verse at a time), and who should do the reading. Is the passage short enough to read the whole of it or should some parts be paraphrased by the teacher? Work through the passage, deciding which points should be raised. Design simple questions to bring out the main teaching of the passage. The first questions should elicit the facts and should be designed so that they cannot be answered by a simple 'no' or 'yes'. If a group member reads out a Bible verse as the answer, praise him/her and then ask ask him/her to put it in his/her own words. Once the facts have been established go on to application questions, encouraging the group to think through how the teaching can be applied to their lives. The 'Question Section' is designed to help you when it comes to discussing the application of the Bible passage.

5. VISUAL AIDS

Pictures are very rarely required for this age group. A Bible Timeline is useful so that the young people can see where the Bible passage they are studying comes in the big picture of God's revelation to his people. You can find one at the back of this book. A map is helpful to demonstrate distances, etc. A flip chart or similar is handy to summarise the lesson.

6. ACTIVITIES AND PUZZLES

These are designed to reinforce the Bible teaching and very little prior preparation (if any) is required by the teacher.

BENEFITS OF ON THE WAY

• Encourages the leaders to study the Bible for themselves.

• Teaches young people Bible-study skills.

• Everything you need is in the one book, so there is no need to buy activity books.

• Undated materials allow you to use the lessons to fit your situation without wasting materials.

• Once you have the entire syllabus, there is no need to repurchase.

On The Way for 11-14s is designed to teach young teens how to read and understand a passage of Scripture and then apply it to their lives (see How to Prepare a Lesson). Before learning how to study the Bible they need to know what it is and how to find their way around it.

The Bible

Christians believe that the Bible is God's word and contains all we need to know in order to live in relationship with God and with each other. It is the way God has chosen to reveal himself to mankind; it not only records historical facts but also interprets those facts. It is not a scientific text book.

What does the Bible consist of?

The Bible is God's story. It is divided into 2 sections - the Old and New Testaments. 'Testament' means 'covenant' or 'promise'.

The Old Testament contains 39 books covering the period from creation to about 400 years before the birth of Jesus. It records God's mighty acts of creation, judgment and mercy as well as their interpretation through the words of the prophets.

The New Testament is made up of 27 books containing details of the life, death and resurrection of Jesus, the spread of the gospel in the early Church, Christian doctrine and the final judgment.

Who wrote the Bible?

The books of the Bible were written by many different people, some known and others not. Christians believe that all these authors were inspired by God (2 Peter 1:20-21, 2 Timothy 3:16). As a result we can trust what it says.

How can we find our way around it?

Each book in the Bible is divided into chapters, each one of which contains a number of verses. When the Books were written originally the chapter and verse divisions were absent. These have been added to enable the readers to find their way around. When written down they are recorded in the following way, Genesis 5:1-10. This tells us to look up the book of Genesis, chapter 5, verses 1 to 10.

At the front of the Bible is a contents page, listing the books in the order in which they come in the Bible. It is perfectly acceptable to look up the index to see which page to turn to.

Aids to teach the Bible passage

*   Many of the lessons have activity pages that help to bring out the main teaching of the Bible passage.
*   Packs of maps and charts can be purchased from Christian book shops.
*   A Bible Time Line is useful to reinforce the chronology of the Bible (see back of this book).

Questions to aid in understanding

Periodically use the following questions to help the young people understand the passage:
*   Who wrote it?
*   To whom was it written?
*   When was it written?
*   What situation is being described? (if applicable)

THE BIBLE LIBRARY

To make a chart of the Bible Library enlarge the template below and photocopy as required. Draw 2 sets of shelves on a large piece of paper (see diagram). Label the shelves. Cut off the unwanted books from each set and write the names of the books on the spines. Glue the books onto the appropriate shelves in the order in which they appear in the Bible.

The Bible Library

Old Testament	New Testament
Law (5 books)	Gospels & Acts (5)
History (12 books)	Paul's Epistles (13)
Poetry & Wisdom (5)	Other Epistles (8)
Prophets (17 books)	Prophecy (1 book)

OVERVIEW
Psalms

SERIES AIMS

1. To understand how knowledge of who God is and what he has done helps me to trust him in every situation.

2. To see how Psalm 22 points forward to the crucifixion.

MEMORY WORK

Show me your ways, O LORD, teach me your paths; guide me in your truth and teach me, for you are God my Saviour, and my hope is in you all day long.

Psalm 25:4-5

Psalms

The Psalter was the hymnbook used in Temple worship following the return from exile. However, the psalms are not merely hymns but are also a means of teaching, e.g. Psalm 34 where each verse begins with a letter of the Hebrew alphabet, and call for a personal response from the hearer. All psalms are addressed to God or speak about him. They speak about the God of Israel, who brought them out of Egypt, made a covenant with them, and who cares for and defends his people. No psalm asks for eternal salvation, although some cry for forgiveness (Psalm 51) and some speak of a future hope. The OT Jew had no developed theology of a final judgment and many of the psalms cry out to God for judgment on the wicked here and now (Psalms 35, 69). The psalms are written from the standpoint of God's people, who had a special relationship with him. The Psalter is split into 5 books and these were used in public worship in conjunction with the 5 books of the Torah (Genesis - Deuteronomy). Each of the 5 sections ends with a doxology.

Book	Psalms	Torah	General comment
I	1-41	Genesis	creation, sin and redemption
II	42-72	Exodus	nation of Israel - ruined and redeemed.
III	73-89	Leviticus	God's holiness, the temple, God on the throne
IV	90-106	Numbers	relationship of Israel and God's Kingdom with surrounding nations
V	107-150	Deuteronomy	God and his word praise hymns

The Psalter was completed and put in order during the time of Ezra, although many of the psalms date from an earlier period, e.g. Psalm 90 (a prayer of Moses), psalms written by David. Almost half the psalms are attributed to David. Many of these are thought to have been written by him, although 'of David' can also mean 'in the manner of' or 'authorised by'. Other authors are Solomon (2), Asaph and the sons of Korah (24), Heman (1), Ethan (1) and Moses (1) leaving 48 unaccounted for. Asaph and the Sons of Korah were groups of temple administrators from the time of Solomon who were responsible for temple worship. Some psalms, e.g. 137, were written during the time of Ezra and the rebuilding of the second temple. Some of the psalms were used on specific occasions, e.g. Psalm 81: Feast of Tabernacles; Psalms 113-118: Passover; Psalms 120-134: Sung by pilgrims on their way to Jerusalem to celebrate the 3 annual festivals; Psalm 130: The Day of Atonement.

When reading the psalms the following points are useful:

1. They were written to Jews. How do today's Jews interpret them, and why do Christians interpret them differently? e.g. Psalm 22 was written by David and gives useful insight into his situation, but the Jew sees no reference to the Messiah. For the Jew, the Messiah is not meant to suffer but will come in glory to reign. The psalms also give the modern Jew help in knowing how to praise and pray to God.

2. Jesus and Peter quoted from them in order to prove the point being made.
e.g. Matthew 21:16 cf. Psalm 8:2; Matthew 21:42 cf. Psalm 118:22-23; Acts 2:25-28 cf. Psalm 16:8-11; Acts 2:34-35 cf. Psalm 110:1. This demonstrates that Jesus and the early church found the psalms useful and authoritative.

3. The following psalms contain references to the Messiah.
The anointed King: Psalm 2:1-2 cf. Acts 4:25-26; Psalm 45:6-7 cf. Hebrews 1:9; Psalm 110:1cf. Luke 20:41-44, Hebrews 1:13
God's Son: Psalm 2:7 cf. Hebrews 1:5
God: Psalm 45:6-7cf. Hebrews 1:9; Psalm 68:18 cf. Ephesians 4:7-8; Psalm 102:25-27 cf. Hebrews 1:10-12
Suffering servant: Psalm 22:1 cf. Matthew 27:50; Psalm 35:19 cf. John 15:25; Psalm 40:6-8 cf. Hebrews 10:5-7; Psalm 41:9 cf. John 13:18; Psalm 69:9 cf. John 2:17; Psalm 118:22-23 cf. Matthew 21:42-44, Acts 4:11; Psalm 118:26 cf. Matthew 23:39.

This series looks at 2 psalms from Book I - Psalms 22 and 25. Both were written by David and cry out to God for help at times of distress. In Psalm 22 David looks back to God's deliverance of his people Israel for assurance that God will help him, whereas in Psalm 25 that assurance is provided by David's knowledge of God's character.

PREPARATION

Psalm 22:1-31

LESSON AIMS

To see how this psalm points forward to the crucifixion.

This is the most frequently quoted psalm in the New Testament and the Gospel writers link it with Christ's passion and death. At one level it is a prayer of David's, a cry from the heart, but at another it is a portrayal of the crucifixion.

It can be divided into 4 sections:

v.1-2,6-8,12-18 Despair because of his own situation and God's seeming lack of help.

v.3-5,9-11 Hope as he remembers God's dealings with his people and with himself in the past.

v.19-21 Cry for help.

v.22-31 Assurance and praise

22:1-2 'Why?' God's servants suffer in a hostile and cruel world. David knew opposition from enemies, but at a deeper level Jesus knew the heavy burden of sin on the cross and the separation from God which that entailed.

22:3-5 Hope because of who God is (he is enthroned) and what he has done (his dealings with his people in the past).

22:6 'Worm' cf. Job 25:6. David is in despair.

22:7-8 Matthew 27:39, Mark 15:29. Used by the Gospel writers of Christ's crucifixion.

22:12,13,16 Bulls, lions, dogs, were all metaphors for David's enemies. Dogs were viewed with contempt in OT times. Wild dogs would live outside the villages and cities and live off the refuse. Dogs, therefore, were seen as unclean and touching them caused defilement.

22:12 Bashan was renowned for its good pasture, therefore its bulls were large and vigorous.

22:16-17 A picture of crucifixion.

22:18 cf. Matthew 27:35.

22:20-21 Prayer for rescue from the enemies mentioned in the earlier verses, but in reverse order - dogs, lions, bulls.

22:22 David declares his praise to the Lord in anticipation of an answer. He believed that praise must follow deliverance as surely as prayer sprang from need, and that this would bring honour to God. This praise was usually offered with thank offerings in the presence of the congregation at the temple.

Some of the great company of believers who would join in the great paean of praise to God for his saving acts are mentioned in the following verses:

22:23 Descendants of Jacob.

22:25 The great assembly.

22:26 The poor and those who seek the Lord.

22:27 The families of the nations.

22:29 The rich and the dying.

22:30 Future generations.

QUESTIONS

1. If we are having difficulties how does this psalm help us?

2. 'Count your blessings, name them one by one.' What lesson does this old chorus have for us?

3. Hannah 'poured out her soul to the Lord' (1 Samuel 1:15) What does that mean? What can it teach us?

Predictions Divide the group into two teams and give each team a name, such as Ducks & Drakes, Rabbits & Ferrets. Line up the 2 teams facing each other approximately 1.5 m. apart. Mark out a safety zone approximately 6-10 m. behind both teams, or as far as possible. Touching the wall can count as a safety zone. Allocate the side of a coin to each team, e.g. Ducks are heads and Drakes are tails.

The leader tosses the coin and calls out the name of the team that won the toss. If Ducks are called out, they turn round and run for safety, pursued by the Drakes. Any Duck tagged by a Drake before reaching safety changes sides. Repeat several times. The largest team at the end of the game is the winner.

At the start of the game, having explained the rules, inform the group that you are able to predict the future. Prior to each toss of the coin predict how many people will be tagged during that turn. Count the number to see how correct was the prediction.

Link into the Bible study by pointing out the inaccuracy of the predictions. Let's look at one of the psalms and see how accurately it portrayed the crucifixion.

Photocopy page 10 for each group member. The remaining word is 'dominion' (v.28).

All the following words from Psalm 22 can be found in letter pairs in the grid. The words read either horizontally, vertically or diagonally and can read backwards or forwards, but the letter pairs will always read from left to right. No letter pair is used more than once. One word on the list has been done to show you. When you have found all the listed words you will be left with a word that tells us why everyone will bow down to the LORD.

ANSWER	FEET	PRAISE	WORM
ASSEMBLY	FORSAKEN	PREY	
CLOTHING	GARMENTS	REMEMBER	
CONGREGATION	HELP	RESCUE	
DELIGHTS	HIDDEN	SAVE	
DESPISED	HONOUR	SAVING	
DIVIDE	INSULT	STRONG	
DOGS	LORD	TONGUE	
DUST	MOCK	VOWS	

NG	ON	TI	GA	RE	NG	CO	EN
LY	VI	ER	SW	AN	TS	PR	AK
MB	FE	SA	LT	EN	CK	AI	RS
SE	ET	PR	RM	SU	MO	SE	FO
AS	ST	GA	EY	DO	IN	VO	HI
LP	HE	RO	MI	UE	WS	DD	TS
DE	RE	NI	NG	NG	EN	GH	HO
SP	ON	ME	CL	TO	LI	NO	UE
IS	DE	OT	MB	DE	UR	SC	LO
ED	HI	VI	ST	ER	RE	RD	SA
NG	WO	RM	DI	DU	DO	GS	VE

What is the remaining word and which verse is it from?

PREPARATION

Psalm 25:1-22

LESSON AIMS

To understand how knowledge of God's character helps me trust him to lead me aright.

Psalm 25 is one of David's and was written at a time of distress. It can be split into 4 stanzas of unequal length containing David's personal requests with the final verse (v.22) being a concluding prayer for God's people.

25:1-3   A prayer for rescue.

25:4-7   A prayer for guidance and pardon.

25:8-15   A reason for confidence that God will do as David requests.

25:16-21 A prayer for pardon and rescue.

25:22   A prayer for God's people.

25:1-2   The prayer for rescue from his enemies.

25:3   Assurance that those who trust in God will never be put to shame. The second part of the verse implies that David's enemies had no cause for their hostility.

25:4   cf. Deuteronomy 10:12-13. This prayer is for general rather than specific guidance ('your ways, your paths').

25:5   In order to walk in God's ways we need to be taught God's truth.

          'My hope' speaks about a confident assurance for the future rather than the normal English usage in 'I hope it will happen', meaning it may or may not.

25:6-7   The basis for pardon is God's mercy and love.

25:11   A person's name denoted his character. LORD is in capital letters and indicates that the Hebrew word used is YAHWEH. This is God's supreme covenant name and is the name he used when speaking with Moses out of the burning bush (Exodus 3:14-15).

          David's reason for confidence is found in the character of God.

25:16-18 David repeats his need of forgiveness.

25:17   In the Bible the heart is the centre of the human spirit and is the wellspring of the emotions, thoughts and actions (see Proverbs 4:23).

25:21   Having been pardoned David needs integrity and uprightness in order to live a life pleasing to God.

QUESTIONS ?

1. What does it mean 'to fear God' (v.14)?

2. List the different things this psalm tells about God. How does this help me trust God for the future?

3. What does this psalm teach about God's guidance? In what aspects of my life should I expect God to guide me? How does he do so?

Who Do You Trust? The aim is for the group members to decide which leader can be trusted. Sit 3 or 4 leaders in different parts of the room. One leader has been instructed to tell the truth always, whereas the remaining leaders are to give a mix of true and false answers. The group members have 5 minutes to question the leaders, following which they must decide which leader is the trustworthy one. This can be done in pairs or as individuals.

Discuss how the group members made their decisions. Link in to how David knew he could trust God for his future.

Photocopy page 13 for each group member.

The answer is 'Rescue'.

Solve the following riddle to discover one of the things David asked God to do.

My first is in truth but never in teach,

My second's in guide and also in reach.

My third is in show and also in ways,

My fourth is in mercy but not in days.

My fifth is in trusts and never in fears,

My sixth is in eyes and also in ears.

My whole is a verb that is plain to see,

It tells what my Saviour has done for me.

OVERVIEW
Paul's Latter Ministery

Week 3	**Teaching God's Word**	*Acts 18:23 - 19:22*
	To learn the importance of teaching God's word completely and accurately.	

Week 3 **Teaching God's Word** *Acts 18:23 - 19:22*
To learn the importance of teaching God's word completely and accurately.

Week 4 **Encountering Opposition** *Acts 19:23-41*
To learn how to study a Bible passage and to understand that faithful proclamation of God's word will result in opposition.

Week 5 **Encouraging the Believers** *Acts 20:1-38*
To learn how Paul encouraged the believers through both his preaching and his way of life.

Week 6 **Enduring Misunderstanding** *Acts 21:1 - 22:29*
To see how Paul endured hardships for the sake of the gospel.

Week 7 **Under Guard** *Acts 22:30 - 23:35*
To see how God used circumstances to place Paul where he wanted him.

Week 8 **Making his Defence** *Acts 24:1 - 26:32*
To see the different reactions to Paul's testimony regarding the truth of the gospel.

Week 9 **Journeying to Rome** *Acts 27:1 - 28:31*
To understand that being a disciple of Jesus is costly.

SERIES AIMS

1. To see God's plan of salvation extending across the known world.

2. To learn more about the early church through Paul's continuing work and witness.

MEMORY WORK

If you suffer as a Christian, do not be ashamed, but praise God that you bear that name.

1 Peter 4:16

Paul's Latter Ministery

The background to Paul and his first two missionary journeys is reviewed in Book 2. In this next series on Paul the third missionary journey is studied, followed by the events leading up to his journey to Rome and his imprisonment there.

The third missionary journey (Acts 18:23 - 21:17), like the previous two, started in Antioch and lasted from AD 53-57. It was centred around the city of Ephesus and was a time of consolidation for the churches. During his travels Paul found time to write the two Corinthian letters (AD 55) and Romans (AD 57). Other letters cannot be dated with certainty, although Galatians may have been written in AD 53 from Ephesus or Macedonia. Before returning to Jerusalem and possible imprisonment, Paul took farewell of the elders of the Ephesian church, reminding them of his ministry to them and exhorting them to keep watch over the church God had placed in their care (Acts 20:17-35).

On Paul's return to Jerusalem he visited the temple where some Jews from Asia (Ephesus?) caused a riot by accusing him of breaking the Mosaic law (Acts 21:27-28). Paul was arrested by the Roman soldiers, but permitted to speak first to the crowd and then to the Sanhedrin. Later, following a tip-off from his nephew, Paul was removed to the garrison at Caesarea for his own safety. There he was imprisoned for 2 years, during which time he had the opportunity to defend himself before King Agrippa and the Roman governors Felix and Festus.

Eventually Paul appealed to Caesar, which was his right as a Roman citizen. He was sent under guard to Rome where he spent two years under house arrest, preaching Christ 'with all boldness and freedom' (Acts 28:31). Whilst in Rome he wrote the Epistles to the Ephesians, Colossians and Philemon, and possibly the one to the Philippians. Paul may have been released in AD 62 and again started to travel, so that perhaps he eventually reached Spain. It may be that 1 Timothy and Titus were written during that time.

Paul's second Roman imprisonment is thought to have been in about AD 67/68 and from his dungeon he wrote 2 Timothy, his final letter. He was probably tried and executed at the hand of the Emperor Nero.

In his last letter Paul wrote of fighting the good fight and finishing the race (2 Timothy 4:7). He was shortly to be executed and was able to look back on 30 years of labour as an apostle (AD 36-66).

PREPARATION

Acts 18:23 - 19:22

LESSON AIMS

To learn the importance of teaching God's word completely and accurately.

18:23 Paul begins his third missionary journey in a similar way to his second, with a trip through Galatia and Phrygia (cf. 16:6). As before, the purpose is pastoral, i.e. to strengthen the disciples.

18:24 Alexandria is in Egypt and was an important city of the Roman Empire with a large Jewish population.

18:25 Apollos knew something about Jesus, but, like John the Baptist, he was still looking forward to the coming of the Messiah and his baptism was based on repentance rather than the finished work of Jesus.

18:26 Apollos, like Paul, went first to the synagogue, where Priscilla and Aquila heard him. They had stayed on at Ephesus when Paul returned to Antioch at the end of his second missionary journey (18:18-19). They took Apollos aside to explain the gospel more fully.

18:27 Achaia was the southern part of Greece and had Corinth as its capital.

19:1-2 The first incident of Paul's 3 year stay in Ephesus is his meeting with followers of John the Baptist.

The Holy Spirit was part of John's teaching (Matthew 3:11-12, Mark 1:7-8, Luke 3:16-17). As these men had not even heard that there was a Holy Spirit, they had probably only heard of a baptism of repentance for the forgiveness of sins (Luke 3:3).

19:6 When the Holy Spirit came upon them they had the same experience as the disciples had at Pentecost (2:4,11) and the Gentiles in Caesarea (10:46-47). This was a confirmation of their conversion to both the converts themselves and the missionaries who witnessed it. These other tongues were known languages (2:4, cf. 2:6-11), not incomprehensible babble.

19:8-9 Paul adopts his usual pattern, going first to the synagogue, then to the Gentiles (Acts 13:14,46-48; 14:1). The lecture hall of Tyrannus was probably available during the hours of 11 am - 4 pm, the hot part of the day when people would not be at work.

19:10 Paul's stay of 2 years and 3 months was the longest stay recorded in any missionary journey. Paul's strategy was to plant churches in key cities which would influence the surrounding areas, (cf. Antioch in Pisidia, 13:14,48-49, and Athens, 17:15).

19:11-12 The city of Corinth was deeply interested in magic and the occult. These and the following verses describe the confrontation between the power of the living God and the power of evil.

19:13-16 As a contrast to the previous story, which could be called 'magic', Luke records the attempt of non-Christian Jews to use the power of God. The name of the Lord Jesus is not a 'key' that can be used to produce a miracle.

19:19 The magic scrolls would have contained formulae and secret information for magical incantations. 50,000 drachmas represented 135 years' wages (1 drachma equalled an average wage for a day).

19:21-22 The success of the church, coupled with Paul's desire to accompany the gifts of the Gentile church (see 24:17), enabled him to make plans to return to Jerusalem, following which he hoped to visit Rome.

QUESTIONS

1. Look at 18:24-28 and 19:1-7. How did John's baptism differ from Paul's gospel? What evidence is there that Apollos and the disciples of John at Ephesus were truly converted after they had been told the gospel?

   Does it matter if people are only taught part of the gospel as long as they 'follow' Jesus? What does this teach about the importance of being able to explain the gospel accurately?

2. Wherever Paul went miracles occurred. Why did God give Paul power to perform miracles? (See Acts 14:3; 19:17,20.)

NB The signs performed by the apostles confirmed the divine nature of the revelation in the days before the NT was complete. We believe what is written because the people of the time saw the miracles and attested to the truth of the gospel.

VISUAL AID

Photocopy the map on page 18 at A3 and use it to fill in Paul's journeys.

FOCUS ACTIVITY

Chinese Whispers   Play a game of Chinese Whispers, making sure that the group know that the object of the exercise is to pass on the message as faithfully and accurately as they can. Sit in a circle and one person whispers a message/sentence to the person on his/her left. This person whispers the message to the person on their left until the message has travelled right round the circle. The person at the end of the message states the message received from being passed round the room and this is compared with the original message to see how accurate it is.

Link in to the Bible study by pointing out the importance of passing on information faithfully and accurately. In today's Bible study we will see why this is important when passing on the good news about Jesus.

ACTIVITY

Photocopy page 19 for each group member. Split the group into units of 2/3 and ask them to go through the activity sheet, working out what is the Biblical gospel. Leave sufficient time to go through their answers so that they have a clear understanding of the gospel by the end of the session.

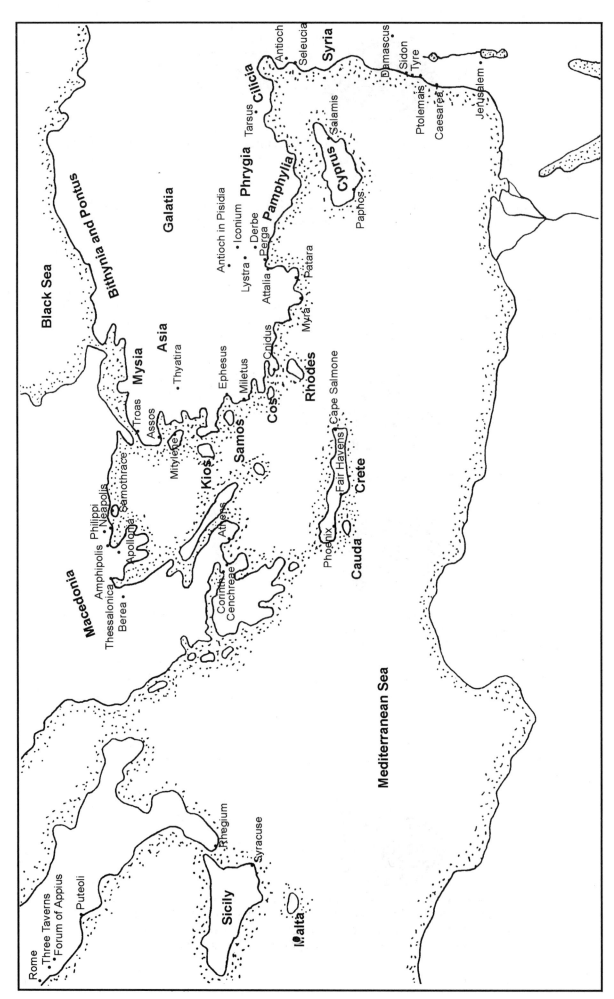

Teaching God's Word — Acts 18:23 - 19:22

When Aquila and Priscilla met Apollos, they discovered that he had only been told a part of the gospel. Could you explain the gospel to a friend? In groups of 2 or 3 look up the Bible verses on this sheet and write down what each one is saying. Then write a simple gospel outline in your own words.

1. Genesis 1:1; 1:31

   Philippians 2:9-11

2. Romans 3:23

   Isaiah 59:2

3. Romans 6:23

4. John 3:16

   1 Timothy 1:15

5. John 3:18

PREPARATION

Acts 19:23-41

LESSON AIMS

To learn how to study a Bible passage and to understand that faithful proclamation of God's word will result in opposition.

This lesson forms part of an occasional series designed to teach the young people how to study the Bible for themselves. Other lessons look at how to study a character (Jacob, Book 1 Week 14 and Joseph, Book 3 Week 7), how to use a concordance to do a word study (Saviour, Book 3 Week 16) and how to study a Bible verse (Book 3 Week 17).

At the beginning of the lesson it is helpful to point out that the Bible is a collection of books and contains different types of literature. Discuss the categories that the Bible books can be broken up into and write them up on the board. Point the group to the index and sort out together where each book fits (see page 22).

Give each group member a copy of page 22 and go through the steps, applying them to Acts 19:23-41.

19:24   Each trade had a guild and Demetrius may have been the guild leader.

Diana was the equivalent in Roman mythology of the Greek Artemis.

19:25   Demetrius' concern was financial.

19:26   Paul must have preached in Ephesus, as he did in Athens, against idolatry (c.f. 17:16-32).

19:27   Demetrius cleverly invokes a socially acceptable argument to bolster his case, rather than relying on the financial argument, which would have only been of concern to the silversmiths. In this way Demetrius involves the whole community.

The temple of the great goddess was the glory of Ephesus. It was 425 feet long and 220 feet wide with 127 white marble columns, 62 feet high and less than 4 feet apart. In this sanctuary was kept the many breasted image which supposedly had dropped from the heavens (? a meteorite).

19:29   Aristarchus later travelled with Paul from Corinth to Jerusalem (20:3-4) and went with him onto Rome (27:1-2).

19:33   We are not sure why Alexander was pushed forward by the Jews. Both Jews and Christians were considered by the Greeks as atheists. Perhaps Alexander was the Jewish spokesman to make sure that the Greeks did not associate Jews with Christians.

19:35-36 The city clerk was the most important local official and the chief executive of the assembly, acting as a go-between for Ephesus and the Roman authorities. His speech was cleverly addressed to appeal to the civic and religious pride of his hearers.

19:38   He did not deny that Demetrius and his followers may have had legitimate concerns, but pointed out the correct legal procedures.

QUESTIONS

1. What was Demetrius' motive(s) for opposing Paul? How did he express his argument?

2. Why does faithful teaching of God's word provoke opposition? Discuss what opposition (if any) members of the group experience at school/home/ socially. What causes the opposition? How should they handle it?

I Disgree! Hand out copies of recent newspapers and ask the group to look through them to find examples of people disagreeing with something someone else has said. The Letters sections of most broadsheets are particularly good at this. Cut out the stories/letters and pin them on a board. Use a highlighter to show where people have disagreed. Discuss why people have bothered to express their opposition.

This introduces the idea of opposition to what people say. Let's see what happened when people in Ephesus heard Paul preaching about Jesus.

This is a good passage to act. Split the group in half and ask them to prepare a play to act to each other. The play can be either the Bible story or a modern adaptation. Each group is responsible for organising themselves. They should appoint a director, who can then decide with his/her group on the script, apportion the parts, etc.

This passage could also be done as a television news report or a newspaper article.

The Bible is made up of 66 different books, 39 in the Old Testament and 27 in the New. The books can be categorised as follows:

1. History   The Jews: Genesis - Esther.

                     Life of Jesus: Matthew - John

                     The Early church: Acts

2. Laws   Exodus - Deuteronomy

3. Poetry   Job, Psalms, Song of Solomon

4. Wisdom sayings   Proverbs, Ecclesiastes

5. Prophecy   Isaiah - Malachi

6. Letters   Romans - Jude

7. Apocalyptic   Daniel, Zechariah, Revelation

How to study a passage

When studying a Bible passage there are certain steps which should be followed.

A   How did the original hearers understand the passage?

1. What is the background/context?

    What is the book about? Use a commentary or dictionary to aid understanding.

    A useful commentary covering the whole Bible is the IVP New Bible Commentary.

2. Who wrote it and why?

3. What kind of writing is it?

a)	History	OT	Where does this episode come in Israel's history?
		Gospels	What is Jesus saying/doing? What response did it evoke?
		Acts	Where does this episode come in the formation of the church?
b)	Laws		What does this say about my relationship with God/other people?
c)	Poetry		How did the speaker feel?
d)	Wisdom sayings		What specific situation is being addressed?
e)	Prophecy		What was wrong with the prophet's society?
			Are there any specific instructions for the hearers?
			Is there anything about the future

                                                          - in OT times?

                                                          - life of Jesus?

                                                          - end of the world?

                     If so, has it been fulfilled?

f)	Letters		Who wrote it and to whom?
			Why was it written?
			What advice was given?
g)	Apocalyptic		What is the central theme?

4.   What is the meaning of individual words and/or verses?
      Use a dictionary or commentary.

B   What is the main teaching of the passage?
      Try and summarise what the passage is about.
      Are there any general principles?

C   Is there a helpful verse or part of a verse?
      This should be to do with the main lesson of the passage.

D   What do I learn about God?
      The Father
      The Son
      The Holy Spirit

E   What do I learn about mankind?
      People generally
      The world
      The church
      The Christian

F   Is there anything to apply to my situation?
      An example to follow
      A command to obey
      A warning to heed
      A promise to trust

PREPARATION

Acts 20:1-38

LESSON AIMS

To learn how Paul encouraged the believers through both his preaching and his way of life.

20:1-2   Everywhere Paul went he encouraged the believers.

Paul wrote both letters to the Corinthians from Ephesus. From these we see that 2 of Paul's aims on leaving Ephesus were to meet Titus in Troas to hear what was happening in Corinth (2 Corinthians 2:12-13) and to continue collecting the offering for the churches in Judea (1 Corinthians 16:1-4).

20:4-5   Many of the names in the list of Paul's companions can be found in the greetings in Paul's letters, e.g. Romans 16:21-23.

20:5-6   'Us' and 'we' suggests that Luke joined Paul at Philippi.

20:6   Troas was the rendezvous for Paul and those who went ahead by sea from Neapolis, the seaport of Philippi. Paul and his immediate companions stayed in Philippi and set sail a few days later.

20:7   The first day of the week was Sunday. This is the first time we read that the Christians met on the first day of the week.

20:8-9   The fumes from the many lamps may have contributed to Eutychus' drowsiness.

20:10   The healing is reminiscent of the miracles of Elijah and Elisha (1 Kings 17:19-22, 2 Kings 4:32-35).

20:11   Undaunted, Paul continues where he left off and they broke bread.

20:13   Assos was on the opposite side of the peninsula from Troas, about 20 miles on foot, 40 miles by sea.

20:18-21   Paul reminds the elders of his conduct and suffering during the 2-3 years he was with them.

20:22-24   Paul was aware of his coming imprisonment and troubles in Jerusalem. For the work God gave him to do, see Acts 9:15-16.

20:25   'None of you will ever see me again' was not a message from God, but what Paul anticipated. It seems that Paul did revisit Ephesus (see 1 Timothy 1:3).

20:26-27   Paul was confident that the completeness of his message absolved him of all responsibility for the fate of his hearers.

20:28-31   Paul gives a solemn charge to the elders. The wolves of v.29 were the false teachers. Note that some of these would come from within the church.

20:33   Paul was quite clear in his teaching that the Christian teacher had a right to be supported by the churches (1 Corinthians 9:4-14), although he usually relinquished that right for himself (2 Thessalonians 3:7-10).

20:35   The weak included those who were not well off, as well as those who were sick.

These words of Jesus are not recorded in any of the gospels, but see John 21:25!

20:36-38   The account of the farewell is emotional. No one could accuse Paul of being a hard, cold, man!

QUESTIONS

1. What does this chapter teach about Paul's main desire? How far had it been achieved? (See Acts 9:15-16 for the task God had given Paul.)

2. Why were Paul's words so important to the early church? What should we learn from this about the importance of daily Bible reading? Discuss ways of doing this.

3. Where was the danger for the early church (20:29-30)? How can we tell the false teachers from the true?

VISUAL AID

Use the map on page 18 to chart Paul's journey. This can be photocopied at A3.

FOCUS ACTIVITY

Word and Action   Play a simple game of charades where one person acts out a single word for the remainder of the group to guess what it is. Prepare a list of words to be acted out. Divide the group into teams. One person from each team is given the first word and acts it out to the team. As soon as the team guesses the word correctly the next member of the team goes to the leader and is given the second word. Continue until all the words have been guessed correctly. The first team to finish is the winner.

Link in to the Bible study by pointing out that it is possible to tell what someone is saying without them actually saying anything. In today's Bible study we will find out what people learned from watching Paul's behaviour as well as from listening to his words.

ACTIVITY

Photocopy page 26 for each group member.

The letters which make up the answers to the 7 clues can be found in the grid below. Each group of 3 letters comes at the end of its word. Cross off the letters as you use them and write the answers in the bottom grid. When this is correctly completed the letters in the outlined column can be rearranged to complete the word missing from your memory verse. The questions are from today's Bible passage. A verse reference is given at the bottom of the page if you need help.

AG	AN	AY	CE	CH	CO	DI
ED	EM	EN	ENT	EP	EU	HE
LE	MI	NT	ORT	PE	PR	RDS
RE	SH	ST	TUS	TY	UR	US

1. As Paul travelled from place to place he spoke words of .... to the believers.

2. What was the name of the young man who fell out of the window?

3. Where did Paul meet the elders of the Ephesian church?

4. What word does Paul use for 'being sorry'?

5. Another word for 'overseers of the flock'. (Jesus was a good one!)

6. What will some men do to the truth after Paul has left the Ephesian church?

7. What did Paul do when he knelt down with the church elders?

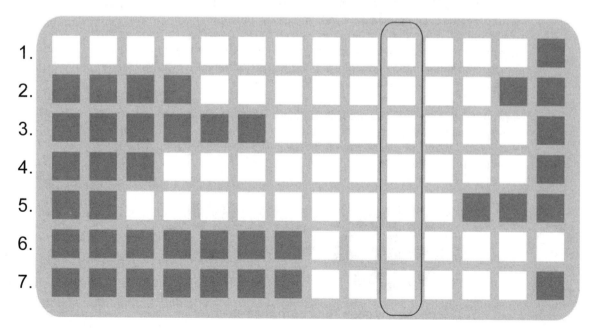

If you suffer as a Christian, do not be .... , but praise God that you bear that name.

1 Peter 4:16

PREPARATION
Acts 21:1 - 22:29

LESSON AIMS
To see how Paul endured hardships for the sake of the gospel.

21:1   Note the first person plural, indicating Luke's presence.

21:3-4   The believers in Tyre probably stemmed from the dispersion following the death of Stephen (Acts 11:19). These believers had been given divine insight into what was to happen to Paul, but had misinterpreted it as a warning to stop Paul proceeding (see also vv.10-12).

21:8   See Acts 6:1-6; 8:1-5,26-40.

21:9   The unmarried daughters may be mentioned to show the passage of time since the events of Acts 8, i.e. a period of some 20 years.

21:18   James was the brother of Jesus, author of the NT letter and leader of the church in Jerusalem.

21:20-24   The leadership was forestalling a problem, as they saw it, by requesting Paul take part in purification rites. It appears that some Jews believed that Paul had been telling the Jews to turn away from Moses, whereas Paul was teaching Gentiles that they need not become Jews in order to be saved.

21:25   James reaffirmed the stand taken in Acts 15:19-20, limiting the burden the Gentiles should take. All these conditions affected either the believer's relationship with God, (food offered to idols, sexual immorality), or his relationship with devout Jewish Christians, (meat with blood in it).

21:27   Jews from Asia had already caused Paul problems (see Acts 20:19).

21:28   Bringing Greeks into the temple area was explicitly forbidden by the temple laws. Any Gentile found there could be killed.

21:30   The gates of the temple were shut to prevent further trouble inside.

21:31   The Roman garrison was housed in the tower of Antonia, overlooking the temple area.

21:40   Aramaic was the most commonly used language amongst Palestinian Jews.

22:2-5   Paul gives his credentials as a Jew. Gamaliel was the most well-known rabbi of the 1st century (see Acts 5:34-40).

22:6-16   The conversion account here differs only slightly from the description in 9:1-31, although Ananias' part in the story is told more fully.

22:17-21   This part of the story is known only from this version. The mention of the Gentiles (v.21) starts the crowd off again.

22:25   'They stretched him out' - this involved tying a person to a whipping post.

Roman citizens were excluded from all degrading forms of punishment such as beating with rods, scourging and crucifixion.

22:28   There were 3 ways to become a Roman citizen:

   a) receive it as a reward for service to Rome,
   b) buy it at great expense,
   c) be born into a family of Roman citizens.

1. Paul knew that by going up to Jerusalem he would face persecution and trouble. Why did he still go?
2. What does this teach us about the presence of hardships in the Christian life? How does this differ from the 'health and wealth' gospel (come to Jesus and all your problems will be solved)?
   NB the problem of suffering is studied in detail in Book 2 Week 25.

VISUAL AID

Use the map on page 18 photocopied at A3.

FOCUS ACTIVITY

Endurance....This is a version of the popular Japanese television show. Contestants (all the members of the group) undertake various endurance tasks, dropping out of the game when they fail a task. The winner is the last person remaining. Possible tasks: **Ski training** - lean against a straight, flat wall with legs at right angles as though sitting on a chair. Hold this position for as long as possible. (You might want to set a time limit.) **Flight training** - hold arms out horizontally to the ground, perhaps holding books for weight. **Press ups** - contestants perform press ups in time until all but one have dropped out. This activity introduces the idea of endurance. Let's see what sort of things Paul endured for the sake of the gospel.

ACTIVITY

A quiz. Divide the group into 2 teams. The first team to get Paul from Ephesus to Jerusalem will be the winner.

Requirements
Each team requires a representational drawing (see diagram) and 8 rectangles of card, 6 with an arrow pointing in the direction of the journey and 2 blank. The pieces of card are randomly numbered from 1 to 8 on the back and pinned to a board with the numbers showing. The 2 blank cards introduce an element of chance, so that a team member who answers a question incorrectly will not place the team in an irretrievable position.

Rules
A question is put to each team in turn and, if answered correctly, one of the team members chooses a card by calling out its number. The card is turned over and, if it has an arrow, is pinned onto the board to show Paul's journey. Blank cards are discarded. If an incorrect answer is given the question is offered to the

other side. You need a total of 16 questions from the Bible passage, 8 for each team. Allow 10-15 minutes for the quiz.

- Ephesus

- Cos

  - Rhodes
    - Patara

        - Tyre

      - Caesarea

          •
          Jerusalem

PREPARATION

Acts 22:30 - 23:35

23:3   Cf. Ezekiel 13:10-12, Matthew 23:27-28. Both Josephus and rabbinic tradition record that Ananias was unworthy of the office of High Priest.

The Levitical law spoke against the perversion of justice. By ordering Paul to be struck the High Priest was passing judgment before Paul had been given opportunity to state his case.

23:5   It is not clear whether Paul did not genuinely recognise the High Priest or whether he was being ironic because Ananias' behaviour had been unworthy of a High Priest. The verse Paul quotes is Exodus 22:28.

23:6   Sadducees did not believe in the resurrection of the dead. Paul's statement caused the rift between the different factions in the Sanhedrin to be demonstrated to the Roman commander. As a result, the commander would be unlikely to pay serious attention to any charge against Paul brought by the Sanhedrin.

23:11   Cf. Acts 18:9-10.

23:14-15   Not all the Sanhedrin were involved.

23:16   We have very little personal information about Paul. It appears that some of his family lived in Jerusalem. We do not know how Paul's nephew heard of the plot.

23:23   Paul was given a large escort. The job of the Roman commander was to keep the peace and prevent any uprising by the Jews. It was important that an attack on Paul did not act as a flashpoint and cause a full scale revolt.

23:24   Felix had been appointed by the Emperor Claudius in AD 52.

23:25-30   Probably the letter's contents would have been read out in court, which would explain Luke's knowledge of its contents.

25:32   The bulk of the armed forces returned to Jerusalem as soon as Paul's safety could be assured.

LESSON AIMS

To see how God used circumstances to place Paul where he wanted him.

QUESTIONS

1. Why were the religious people of Paul's day so opposed to the truth?

2. Do people really want to know the truth? If they did what would it show up? Look up John 3:16-21.

3. Look up Acts 9:15-16. Has Paul completed the job God gave him to do? To which group has he yet to preach? How have the circumstances in today's passage served to forward the spread of the gospel?

VISUAL AID

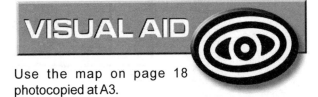

Use the map on page 18 photocopied at A3.

FOCUS ACTIVITY

Remote Control   Divide the group into pairs with one member of each pair blindfolded. Give the pairs a task to perform, such as collecting a cup of water, walking around the room, opening a door, etc. The blindfolded person must perform the task by listening to directions given by his partner.

Link in to the Bible study by pointing out that the blindfolded people were controlled by people who could see the big picture. Let's see how God controlled circumstances to place Paul where he wanted him.

ACTIVITY

Photocopy page 30 for each group member.

In this puzzle, the answers to the clues are entered in the grid in a clockwise direction around the spiral. Each answer starts from its clue number and the last letter of one answer is the first letter of the next one. The answers can be found in today's Bible passage.

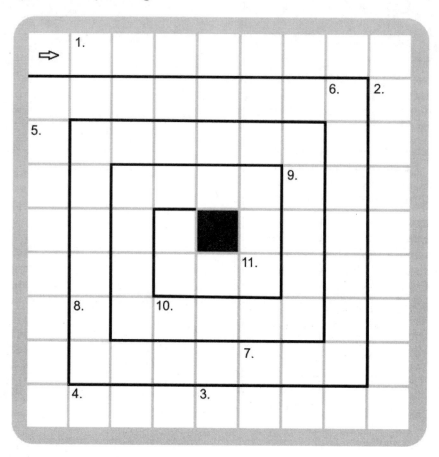

1.   Who ordered the chief priests and Sanhedrin to assemble? (22:30)

2.   For what belief did Paul say he was on trial? (23:6)

3.   On which morning did the Jews form a conspiracy? (23:12)

4.   Some Pharisees were .... of the law. (23:9)

5.   Which group of Jews did not believe in the resurrection? (23:8)

6.   What was the name of the Jewish ruling council? (23:1)

7.   Who told Paul about the plot? (23:16)

8.   What sort of wall did Paul call the High Priest? (23:3)

9.   What became violent in 23:10?

10. What did the Jews promise not to do in 23:12 (3,2,5)?

11. What did the Jews want to do to Paul? (23:12)

PREPARATION

Acts 24:1 - 26:32

LESSON AIMS

To see the different reactions to Paul's testimony regarding the truth of the gospel.

This lesson studies 3 hearings before important officials. It is a long passage and parts of it will need to be paraphrased.

24:1-26 Paul's trial before Felix

24:1   Five days was the time required for a messenger to go from Caesarea to Jerusalem, for the Sanhedrin to appoint their representatives and for the appointees to return to Caesarea.

        Tertullus was possibly a Hellenistic Jew, familiar with the procedures of a Roman court.

24:2-3   It was accepted practice to start by acknowledging the judge's authority. There had been revolts during Felix's term as Governor and troublemakers had been dealt with severely. Felix was recalled to Rome two years later to answer to the charge of 'misrule' (see 24:27).

24:5   Tertullus' argument has been that Felix has ensured peace and stability by his severe treatment of troublemakers. Paul is also a troublemaker and should be dealt with accordingly.

24:6   The charge of desecrating the temple is only relevant in that it explains the cause of the uproar when Paul was arrested.

24:11-12 Paul answered each accusation. He was not a troublemaker and he had not been involved in causing disturbances.

24:14-16 Paul argued that the beliefs of the Christian Jew need be no less Jewish than the beliefs of the Sadducees and Pharisees.

24:19   This was a new line in his defence. It was commonly accepted that the person bringing charges should be in court to prosecute. Also, if the offences took place in Asia, they were outside Felix's jurisdiction.

24:22   Felix was well acquainted with The Way. He had been governor for six years which was time enough to learn all about Christians. Also, his wife Drusilla was Jewish. She was Felix's 3rd wife, the daughter of Herod Agrippa I. She married Felix when she was 16 and had a son also named Agrippa, who died in the eruption of Vesuvius (AD 70).

24:23   The case against Paul had not been proved. The right course of action would have been to free Paul.

24:26   Not only did Felix demonstrate a complete disregard for justice, he was also avaricious.

25:1-12 Paul's trial before Festus

25:1   Festus died in office after only 2 years, but his record shows him to have been superior in wisdom and honesty to his predecessor.

25:9   Festus was not willing to find Paul innocent, in spite of the inability of the Jews to substantiate their case against Paul. His decision smacks of political expediency (cf. the reaction of Pilate, Luke 23:4,14,20-25).

25:12   Apparently every Roman citizen possessed the right to appeal to Caesar in certain circumstances. Festus was probably greatly relieved to avoid making a final decision about Paul.

25:13 - 26:31 Paul before Festus and Agrippa

25:13   The king and his wife had come on a state visit to the newly appointed Festus.

25:14   King Agrippa was familiar with Judaism and was responsible for appointing the High Priest (see 26:3).

25:25   See 25:9.

25:26   Festus had to write a report on Paul's case, outlining the charges against him, to send with him to Caesar. He needed Agrippa's help to compile something.

26:27   'Do you believe the prophets?' Agrippa was faced with a dilemma. If he replied 'yes', Paul would press him into acceptance of Jesus as a fulfilment of the prophets; if 'no', he would offend the Jews who believed the words of the prophets to be the word of God.

26:28   His question avoided answering Paul.

26:31   The innocence of Paul is obvious to the king. It was only Paul's appeal to Caesar that kept him in chains (v.29), since to free him now would be to usurp the Emperor's power.

1. Look at the reaction of Felix (24:25-26), Festus (25:9-12; 26:24) and Agrippa (26:28,30-32) to Paul's testimony. Why do you think each one reacted in that way?

2. When Paul was asked to give the reason for the hope he had he was able to do so (1 Peter 3:15). If we were asked to give a testimony/explain what we believe could we do so? Discuss a simple gospel outline (see week 3) and practice explaining the gospel to each other.

Action - Reaction Read out a number of scenarios where people are required to react and where there is a choice of reaction. After each scenario ask the group members to indicate how they would react, perhaps by raising a hand or standing up or moving to a particular part of the room. The scenarios must involve being told something - news, information, joke, etc.
Possible scenarios:

1.   You are waiting in a cinema queue and you hear a rumour that the film you want to see is sold out. Do you:

a)   wait in the queue anyway just to make sure?
b)   go home and try to see the film another night?

2.   Somebody approaches you on the street and tells you that they will pay you £5 if you sing them a song. Do you:

a)   sing the song and pocket the £5?
b)   tell them to get lost and leave as fast as you can?

3.   Someone tells you something about one of your friends. Do you:

a)   tell them that they should not be talking about one of your friends behind their back?
b)   thank them for the information and pass it on to the next person you see?

Link in to the Bible study by pointing out that people's reactions vary. Let's see how the authorities reacted to what Paul had to say at his trials.

PREPARATION
Acts 27:1 - 28:31

LESSON AIMS
To understand that being a disciple of Jesus is costly.

These chapters are mostly narrative and require a good deal of reading. It might be helpful to divide the passage up into small sections, read it, discuss it, and then go onto the next section. A map is essential for this lesson (see p.18).

27:1   'We' begins again. It is likely that Luke spent the two years of Paul's imprisonment nearby in Caesarea.

27:2   Aristarchus - see Acts 19:29; 20:4, Colossians 4:10.

27:3   The centurion's friendship stood Paul in good stead on more than one occasion (see also v.42-43).

27:6   They changed ships at Myra. This was a grain ship from Egypt run by the Imperial authorities.

27:7-8   With difficulty they arrived off the town of Cnidus, but then the winds forced them south to Crete. Sailing the Mediterranean was dangerous after mid-September and impossible after mid-November.

27:9   The Fast was the Jewish feast of Atonement, which fell in late September/early October. That year (AD 59) it was October 5th, so they were now between October 5th and November 11th. The Romans considered sailing in November to be suicidal.

27:12   Phoenix served as a major city and wintering harbour with protection against storms.

27:14   Before they reached Phoenix they were caught by hurricane winds blowing from Mount Ida in Crete.

27:17   They tacked carefully to avoid the sand banks off the coast of Libya (evidenced by underwater archaeologists).

27:23   cf. 23:11.

27:31   If the sailors had been allowed to desert the ship the passengers would have been unable to beach the ship the following day.

27:38   By lightening the ship it could go further into shore.

27:42   If a prisoner escaped, the life of his guard was taken in his place (cf. Acts 16:27).

28:11   The sailing season restarted in late February or early March.

28:14   Either the centurion had business to take care of, or he was free to delay the journey at Paul's request.

28:16   As Paul had not committed a major crime he was granted this privilege, but he always had a guard with him (see Ephesians 6:20, Philippians 1:13-14, Philemon 10,13).

28:22   The Jews in Rome were aware of the claims of Jesus to be the Messiah. They wanted to hear Paul's version before the arrival of the 'official' version from the Jewish leaders in Jerusalem.

28:30   For two whole years Paul was able to serve the Lord in this way (v.31). There are several indications that he was released from prison after this time:

     a) Acts stops abruptly,

     b) Paul wrote to the churches expecting to visit them in the near future, so he must have anticipated his release (Philippians 2:24, Philemon 22),

     c) a number of details in the Pastoral letters do not fit into the historical account of Acts, e.g. a return to Crete, Greece and Asia Minor,

     d) tradition indicates that Paul went to Spain.

1. Look at the way Paul used his time on this trip to Rome and in Rome itself. What does this show us about his use of time and talents? What lessons can we learn about the way we use our time and talents?

2. Summarise all the difficulties Paul had to endure in these 2 chapters. How did he behave in difficult circumstances? What can we learn from this about the way to cope with problems?

Trace Paul's journey, using the map on page 18 photocopied at A3.

Follow the Leader The object of the exercise is to follow the leader exactly. This can be done using slow motion actions by a leader standing at the front and people dropping out when they get it wrong, or by a leader leading the way around an obstacle course made from chairs, tables, cups of water, etc.

Link in to the Bible study by pointing out that following someone is not always easy. Let's see how hard it was for Paul to follow Jesus.

Photocopy page 34 for each group member.

The answer to each question begins with the given letter of the alphabet. Try to answer the questions without looking up the Bible verses; these are given to help you if you get stuck.

A............................ The place Paul spent time between his missionary journeys (18:23).

B............................ Sopater came from there (near Thessalonica) (20:4).

C............................ Where Philip the evangelist lived (21:8).

D............................ He was a silversmith (19:24).

E............................ Where the goddess Artemis was worshipped (19:28).

F............................ He was a Roman Governor (23:24).

G............................ The name of the Rabbi Paul studied under (22:3).

H............................ The 2nd half of the name of a harbour on Crete (27:8).

I............................ The country of Paul's final destination (27:1).

J............................ Where Paul performed purification rites (21:17-24).

K............................ An island off the coast of Asia (20:15).

L............................ The doctor who accompanied Paul and wrote Acts. (2 Timothy 4:11)

M............................ Where Paul met the elders of the Ephesian church (20:17).

N............................ The state of dress of the 7 sons of a Jewish priest, when they ran out of the house after a beating by an evil spirit (19:16).

O............................ Another name for the elders of a church (20:28).

P............................ The wife of Aquila (18:26).

Q............................ The way Paul spoke to the disciples who had not heard about the Holy Spirit (19:2-3).

R............................ Where Paul was imprisoned at the end of Acts. (20:14)

S............................ The name of the Jewish chief priest with 7 sons (19:14).

T............................ One of Paul's companions (he came from Lystra) (19:22).

U............................ The name of a Jewish feast (20:6).

V............................ It came out of the fire and bit Paul (28:3).

W............................ An early name for Christianity (19:9).

EX............................ Aquila and his wife did this to Apollos about the way of God (18:26).

Y............................ The age of the man who fell out of the window (20:10).

Z............................ Paul was this for God (22:3).

OVERVIEW Colossians

Week 10	**Introduction**	*Colossians 1:1-14*

To understand that God gives every believer the knowledge and power needed to live the Christian life.

Week 11 | **Fullness in Christ** | *Colossians 1:15 - 2:5*

To understand that full salvation comes through Christ alone. There are no blessings beyond, or outside of, this.

Week 12 | **Freedom in Christ** | *Colossians 2:6-23*

To understand that true Christian freedom is found in Christ alone, not in keeping man-made observances.

Week 13 | **Life in Christ** | *Colossians 3:1-17*

To understand how a Christian should conduct himself in his relationship with Christ and with the local church.

Week 14 | **Relationships in Christ** | *Colossians 3:18 - 4:18*

To learn how Christians should conduct themselves in the area of everyday relationships.

SERIES AIMS

1. To understand that, in Jesus, the believer has been given everything necessary for salvation and godliness.

2. To help us lead lives worthy of our calling as Christians.

MEMORY WORK

You have been given fullness in Christ, who is the Head over every power and authority.

Colossians 2:10

Colossians

Paul wrote this letter to the church at Colosse during his first imprisonment in Rome, where he spent at least 2 years under house arrest (Acts 28:16-31). The letter, along with the one to Philemon, can be dated around AD 60-61.

Several hundred years earlier, Colosse had been a leading city in Asia Minor (present day Turkey). It was located on the Lycus River and on an important east - west trade route from Ephesus, on the Aegean Sea, to the Euphrates River. By the first century AD, Colosse had become relatively unimportant because the trade route had been resited further to the west. Colosse was situated near the towns of Hierapolis and Laodicea (4:13,16).

The gospel was taken to Colosse by Epaphras, who probably had been converted during Paul's 3 year ministry in Ephesus (1:7-8; 4:12, Acts 19:8-10). The young church seems to have consisted of mainly Gentile converts, (2:21 suggests a pagan background), and Paul's letter implies that false teachings were gaining credence. This prompted Epaphras to report the situation to Paul in Rome. Paul sent the letter back to Colosse with Tychicus and Onesimus (4:7-9). Onesimus was an escaped slave, (an offence punishable by death under Roman law), who had fled to Rome where he met Paul and was converted. He and Tychicus also took a letter to Philemon (Onesimus' former master), in which Paul asks Philemon to accept him back as a Christian brother (Philemon 15-16).

Paul's purpose in writing was to refute the Colossian heresy, which is never explained fully in the letter. From the statements Paul makes, it appears that some leaders were teaching the young church a spirituality which was in tune with current secular thinking (2:8). The new Christians were being offered a system of achieving a 'fullness' in their religious experience which was outside the bounds of what had been achieved by their salvation (2:9-23). The main thrust of the letter is to reaffirm the complete adequacy of Christ as contrasted with the emptiness of mere human ideas or philosophy.

PREPARATION

Colossians 1:1-14

LESSON AIMS

To understand that God gives every believer the knowledge and power needed to live the Christian life.

Start the lesson with a brief explanation of how the church at Colosse was started and its situation at the time of writing.

These fourteen verses can be divided into 3 sections:

v.1-2   Greeting
v.3-8   Thanksgiving and reassurance
v.9-14 Prayer for knowledge and power.

It might be worth reading the passage with the group section by section and discussing each one before moving on to the next. Do make sure you draw the whole passage together at the end of the lesson.

Greeting

1:1   By stating his apostleship Paul is emphasising his official authority. This was important if Paul was to reassure the believers that they had received the complete gospel. An apostle had the authority to teach (1 Timothy 2:7) and to deal with the congregation in his care (2 Corinthians 13:10). Both Paul's calling and ministry were by the will of God (Acts 9:15-16, Galatians 1:1). Paul's particular responsibility was for Gentile congregations.

Timothy was not the joint author but had been with Paul during much of the Ephesian ministry (the period of the founding of the Colossian Church) and was with Paul for much of his time in prison.

1:2   Holy means set apart for God and for his service. 'In Christ' is normally used to refer to the sphere in which Christians live.

Grace and peace - cf. Romans 5:1-2.

Thanksgiving and reassurance

1:3-5   With the exception of Galatians, all Paul's letters begin with thanks and praise. By writing about their faith, love and hope Paul is reassuring them that they are real Christians (cf. Romans 5:1-5). None of these three virtues are naturally occurring. All are God-given, and thus demonstrate the genuineness of their Christian profession.

1:4   Love for their fellow-Christians is the outworking of faith in Christ. The love that is a genuine mark of their standing in Christ is love for other Christians, not warm feelings. Both faith and love are based on hope, which means here 'the content of hope', or the 'thing one hopes for'. Christians can be confident about the blessings that will be received in heaven, of which our present experience is but a foretaste. This is further reassurance for the Colossians regarding the genuineness of their Christian belief. They need pay no heed to teachers who tell them that they should receive the complete Christian blessings in the present life.

1:5-6   The gospel they have received is the true gospel, there is no need for a further revelation. It is the same gospel as that received by all the other churches.

1:6   'All over the world' is not meant literally, but is a hyperbole, dramatising the rapid spread of the gospel. The gospel is bearing fruit and growing, it does not need further enrichment.

1:7-8   The Colossians had never met Paul, so needed reassurance that Epaphras had given them the complete message.

Prayer for knowledge and power

1:9   It appears that the new teachers were offering further knowledge to enable the believer to experience greater blessings. Being 'in the know' would mean being part of an inner circle of the spiritually elite. Note the use of 'all'. Paul is pointing out that full knowledge comes from God and they do not need a further initiation from the new teachers.

Biblical knowledge is not just head knowledge but results in practical outworking.

1:10-12   In order to lead a God-pleasing life **every** believer needs **all** God's wisdom. The goals described in these verses are for every believer.

1:11   Paul prays for the Christians to be given fullness of power. Note that the power is not given so that the believer can perform mighty acts or miracles, but for endurance and patience. The result will be a joyful giving of thanks to the Father. This sort of joy, when the believer is under pressure, is not a natural phenomenon.

1:12-14   Paul ends his prayer for the Colossian Christians by thanking God for what is **already** theirs - redemption and forgiveness of sins. They were already qualified to share in the inheritance of the saints, so should not allow anyone to suggest otherwise (2:8).

1. From these verses, what appear to be the problems facing the Colossian church?

2. How does Paul start to answer the questions raised by the false teachers?

3. Why should the Colossians listen to Paul (v.1-2)?

Swamp Things   Set up markers on the floor on each side of the room about 10 paces apart, to create a 'swamp' in which you cannot stand. Allocate the young people to groups of 3 or 4, depending on the size of the group, and give each team 2 or 3 cushions/mats/pieces of newspaper. (Each team is given 1 less item than there are team members.) These items act as 'floats', which the team members can use to stand on in the swamp. The aim is to get the whole team from 1 marker to the far marker as quickly as possible, only using the floats to stand on.

Link in to the Bible study by pointing out that everyone received all they needed to make the journey successfully - they had sufficient equipment. In the same way every believer in Jesus has everything they need to keep going as a Christian, which is what Paul is reminding the Colossians about in this letter.

Photocopy page 40 for each group member. The theme is 'freedom'.

Write the words of the Bible verses below into the grid, starting with the longest words. When you have finished, take the letters from the shaded squares and rearrange them to discover one of the themes of the Letter to the Colossians.

For he has rescued us from the dominion of darkness and brought us into the kingdom of the Son he loves, in whom we have redemption, the forgiveness of sins.
Colossians 1:13-14

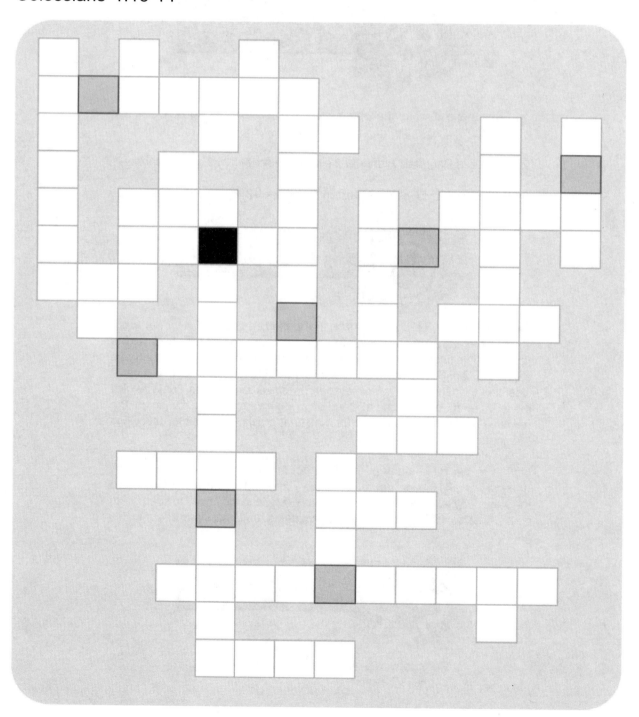

PREPARATION

Colossians 1:15 - 2:5

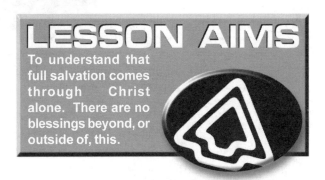

LESSON AIMS

To understand that full salvation comes through Christ alone. There are no blessings beyond, or outside of, this.

1:15   Paul starts this section of the letter with an exposition of the supremacy of Christ and his sufficiency as Saviour, as this knowledge will be the new converts' best defence against being swayed by false teaching.

The image of the invisible God refers to the incarnation (see John 1:14-18). If a person wants to know God he/she needs to find out about Jesus, for he shows us perfectly what God the Father is like.

The firstborn son had all the privileges and family rights, as does Jesus in relation to the whole of creation; priority, pre-eminence and sovereignty.

1:16   Cf. John 1:3, Hebrews 1:2-3. It is not necessary to try and distinguish between thrones, powers, rulers and authorities. The important thing is Jesus' lordship over the whole created order, both material and spiritual. As Jesus is Lord over all spiritual powers he does not need their help to bring his followers full salvation (cf. 2:17).

1:17   As the pre-existent one (John 8:58) Jesus is Lord of the universe. He is also the sustainer of the universe, and apart from his continuous activity all would fall apart (cf. Hebrews 1:2-3).

1:18   Having demonstrated Christ's lordship over creation, Paul moves on to his lordship over the new creation, the church. Because both our physical and spiritual existence come from Jesus, we are foolish to try and separate our lives into secular and sacred areas.

Jesus is the head of the body, the church, and his word tells us all we need for full salvation. We should not listen to any authority that teaches anything different. If

the body cuts itself off from its head it will die!

1:19   Through Jesus God has come to dwell with man. Jesus is the one in whom all fullness can be found, so there is no need to follow the new teachings with their prescriptions for holy living (cf. 2:8,16-17,20-23). We do not need a supplementary work of God to bring us to a full spiritual experience.

1:20   The death of Jesus is the only way we, along with the rest of creation, can be reconciled to God. At the Fall the natural harmony between God and man and creation was destroyed, but this process was reversed when Christ died. Therefore, reconciliation is an accomplished fact, not something we are waiting for. Note that reconciliation comes from God and is directed towards God; there is nothing man can do to bring it about. This verse does not speak of universal salvation. Other Scriptures speak of eternal hell and make clear that only believers are saved.

1:21   The description of the Colossian Christians, as being formerly alienated from God, suggests they were Gentiles (cf. Ephesians 2:11-12). This verse points out the importance of the mind as being the place where evil behaviour starts. By contrast see Romans 12:1-2.

1:22   Note the contrast with verse 21. All this has been brought about solely by Christ's death on the cross. The new converts required no second blessing.

1:23   Paul is not implying that salvation, once gained, can be lost, rather that continuing in the faith demonstrates our standing as believers. Like a building set on foundations, so Christians must not shift from the sure

41

foundation of the gospel. This gospel was the one they had originally heard, the one preached to all the other churches (universal) and the one Paul preached (apostolic). There is no room here for a different gospel.

1:24   By calling on the Colossian Christians to remain loyal to the gospel he preached, Paul is also calling them to remain loyal to himself. So it is important for him to set out his credentials. Possibly the new teachings were effective because of the charisma of the teachers (cf. 2:4). These new teachings set out to complete what was lacking in the believers' spiritual experiences. Probably, the teachers pointed to various experiences as hallmarks of their authority, experiences that Paul was lacking. Paul points to his sufferings as the genuine hallmark of a minister of the gospel, and, as such, he is able to rejoice in them. He is not stating that his sufferings added anything to Christ's sufferings in effecting reconciliation.

1:25   Paul's ministry involved serving the church as well as serving the gospel (v.23). Faithful preaching of the word of God is an essential. We can only know Jesus better by knowing the Scriptures better. This is hard work and there are no short cuts! However, we can be encouraged by the fact that the Lord gives understanding (2 Timothy 2:7). Paul has told them the complete word of God, they do not need anything extra. (They did not have the NT as yet.)

1:26   At that time, mystery religions were in vogue, each one offering its own initiation into the secret of life. The mystery is the gospel of Christ (v.27) and is for all believers, not just the privileged few. It had to be revealed by God, so cannot be discovered by men.

1:27   'Christ in you' speaks of the indwelling of the Holy Spirit (Ephesians 3:14-19). The Spirit's work is to bring the believer all the blessings achieved through Christ. Possibly the new teaching was that the Holy Spirit would bring extra blessings to the life of the believer and this is why Paul wrote of 'Christ in you' rather than the Holy Spirit in you.

The hope of glory speaks of reassurance.

The Holy Spirit is our assurance of salvation and eternal life (2 Corinthians 1:21-22). We will only fully experience the blessings God has provided when we get to heaven.

1:28   Paul was prepared to rebuke error as well as to teach truth. The two should go together.

'Present' was a word used in legal language and means 'to bring someone before a court' (see also v.22). In Christ is found everything that is needed for salvation and godly living. No one needs anything else.

1:29   Paul is only able to fulfil the ministry of v.28 through God's power working in him. 'Power' was another hallmark of the new teachers. Paul points out that this power is given as he is working, not by 'receiving it through faith'. It is as Paul works hard at the job God has given him, that he receives the energy he needs to do that job. The power Paul is talking about is the power that raised Jesus from the dead (2:12). From this verse it does not appear that Paul experienced any spiritual ecstasy at having God's power at work within him. The verbs used speak of agonising toil. The evidence of God's power at work was the work being done, not some mystical experience.

2:1   Because Paul had never met the Christians at Colosse it was easy for wrong impressions to be given regarding his concern for them (see also v.5).

Laodicea was 11 miles away.

2:2   Paul encourages unity, knowing that the result of the new teaching will be divisiveness because of its emphasis on a spiritual elite. Paul's purpose is that the church will have the full riches of complete understanding. He does not want them to have second best.

2:4   Even though the new teachers were not teaching the truth, people got carried away because of their eloquence, and so did not recognise the flaws in their argument.

QUESTIONS

1. How would you answer a Christian friend who tells you that you need a further experience, which will allow you to experience God's presence and power in a new way? Trace Paul's argument through 1:15-20 and put it in your own words.

2. Read through the whole passage, picking out every time 'all' is used. How does the use of this word affect Paul's argument? What confidence does this give you regarding your position as a child of God?

FOCUS ACTIVITY

Stuck Together   Divide the group into pairs, holding hands or wrists. One person is 'It', who catches people by touching them on the shoulder. Anyone who is caught remains stuck to the spot and is separated from their partner. They can only be freed if their partner crawls through their legs, then they become a pair again. The game ends when everyone is stuck or when 'It' tires!

Link in to the Bible study by pointing out that once you have been caught there is only one way you can be reconciled to your partner and continue the game. Let's see what Paul says about all you need to be reconciled with God.

ACTIVITY

Photocopy page 44 for each group member. The text is Colossians 2:10.

Fit the jigsaw pieces into the frame provided to discover something about the status of the Christian. There are no gaps between words and the shaded squares are to help you get started.

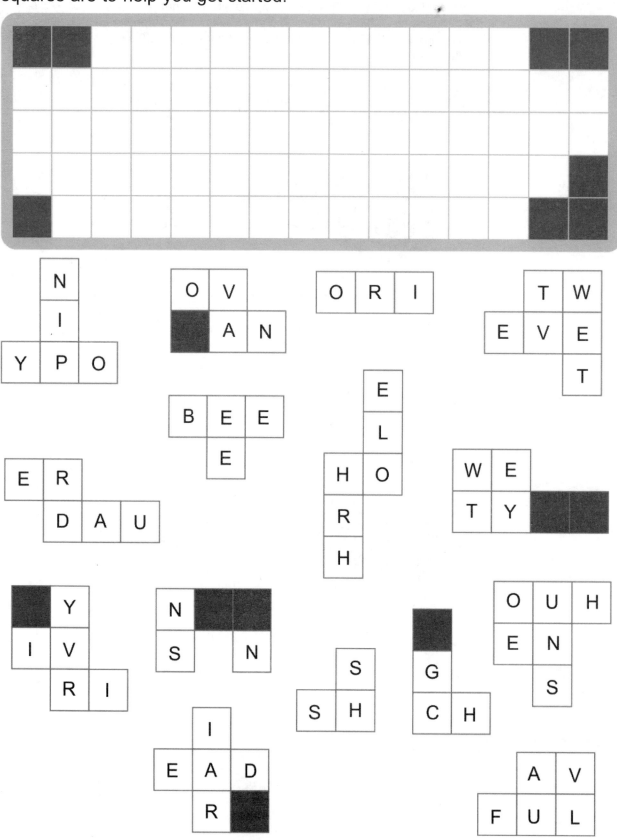

This text comes later on in chapter 2.   Which verse is it?

PREPARATION

Colossians 2:6-23

LESSON AIMS

To understand that true Christian freedom is found in Christ alone, not in keeping man-made observances.

It would be helpful to have a flip chart or board for this lesson. Start by summarising what you have learned so far about the new teachers, their teachings and how Paul has argued against them. This can be done in table form and can be added to as this lesson progresses. This should help to clarify Paul's argument for the group and also help in the application.

2:6 'Received Christ' means received the apostolic gospel. When we acknowledge Jesus as Saviour we also acknowledge him as Lord. It is only because he is Lord over Satan and all his works that he is able to deliver us from sin. Living as a Christian means acknowledging Jesus' right to deliver us from sinful living (which we quite enjoy!), not just from the penalty of sin. Conversion should lead to worthy living (1:10) and Christians should be continually growing.

2:7 'Rooted and built up' refers to the Christian foundation, which is Christ. We should not seek to grow in an element different from the one where we were planted.

The way we will continue to be strengthened in the faith is through the apostolic gospel. Thankfulness should be a hallmark of true Christian spirituality.

2:8 Although the new teachers were promising spiritual fullness and freedom, in reality they were placing the Colossian Christians in bondage. The word used for philosophy means a deep knowledge of spiritual mysteries. The basic principles of the world are the powerful ideas which come through human traditions and the current climate of opinion (cf. Galatians 4:3,8-10). By claiming to lead men to a 'full' knowledge of God these principles are very seductive. They are deceptive because they are religious, e.g. the need for a special leader to preside over the church service, a special place for the church service, a special initiation ceremony. The world has no difficulty with this concept because it is what the world means by 'religion'. This was the basis of the new teachers' authority.

2:9 The word used for dwells implies God coming to be with man. If all God's fullness dwells in Jesus, then he is the only source of it, so we should not look for it elsewhere.

2:10 'You have been given' is past tense. The believer already possesses fullness, so does not need to go elsewhere for it.

2:11 It may be that the new teachers were urging physical circumcision as a special mark of dedication, bringing with it a second blessing of freedom from sin in all its forms. Christian circumcision is spiritual, involving a shedding of the sinful nature, not the physical shedding of the foreskin.

2:12 By being buried with Christ the Christian shares in his death. Jesus' death took God's judgement on sin, therefore the Christian is no longer under God's condemnation. It does not mean that sin in our lives has been put to death. Note that Paul uses the past tense again. The benefits are already ours. The power that raised Jesus from the dead is already at work in the Christians' lives, so why seek for it through man-made observances?

2:13 This implies that the Colossians were probably Gentiles not Jews. God is the only author of salvation.

2:14 All mankind is under obligation to keep God's law, a debt none can pay. God cancelled the debt through the cross. When a criminal was crucified, a list of his crimes was nailed to his cross.

2:15   The cross does not just bring deliverance from sins, but also deliverance from the powers of this world (Satan is the prince of this world, John 14:30, Ephesians 2:2). When Roman generals returned from the wars they brought their disarmed foes back in a victory procession so that everyone would know they had been victorious.

2:16   God is our only judge. It appears the new teachers were saying the marks of true spirituality were missing in the Colossian church. The marks mentioned can be split into 2 groups, things to do without and things which must be done. The new teachers were going beyond OT observance (there is nothing in the Mosaic law about drink) and instituting their own rules. Elsewhere Paul teaches the importance of self-discipline if time is to be found for prayer, Bible reading, etc. (e.g. 1 Corinthians 9:24-27). In the case of marriage, alcohol, etc. abstinence is personal and voluntary, not compulsory (1 Timothy 4:1-5). Christ is the Creator, so why refuse the blessings he has created? As well as stating things a 'truly spiritual' Christian should do without, the new teachers also stipulated special services and rituals which must be observed.

2:17   All the feasts and sacrifices in the OT are referred to as shadows (Hebrews 8:1-13) because they pointed forward to the coming of Christ, so to return to those laws would be a retrograde step. By living in the shadows, the new teachers were actually inferior to the Colossian Christians, not superior.

2:18   The word used for false humility implies some kind of mortification and self denial, e.g. excessive fasting. This may have been needed to put the body in a state to receive visions (low blood sugar?).

Worship of angels does not refer to worship directed to angels. Some commentators suggest it means employing angels as intercessors. This would fit with the false humility that says man is too bad to approach God through Christ alone. It could also mean angel-like worship, the worship (of God) which angels perform. If that is the case the false teachers were claiming to have joined in angelic worship of God, possibly using special angelic language.

The new teachers were basing their authority on their visions and spiritual experiences rather than on God's word. Jesus is the only one who speaks truthfully about heaven as he is the only one to have come down from heaven (John 3:11-13). The root of the problem is spiritual pride and the result is division within the church.

2:19   Paul levels a devastating criticism at those who use their own private religious experiences as the basis for their authority. That person is not superspiritual, as he imagines, but has lost contact with Christ.

2:20-21   See v.8. Being enslaved to the religious principles of this world does not bring freedom.

2:22   This verse suggests the rules to be kept were not the Mosaic law but new ones, imposed by the new teachers. Although the new teachers were offering the Colossian Christians freedom from the Law, in reality they offered enslavement to a new law.

2:23   The new teachings sounded impressive, but they were powerless to control sinful behaviour.

QUESTIONS

1. In this passage what does Paul say the Christian has been freed from? What is the Christian freed for? How does this differ from the new teaching at Colosse?

2. In what sense are we 'free' in Christ? Does this mean we do not need to keep the OT Law? (cf. Romans 6:1-14).

3. In what ways are Christians tempted to live in the shadows today (v.16-17)?

FOCUS ACTIVITY

New Rules   Play a simple game where everyone is familiar with the rules. As the game progresses, gradually add in more rules to make the game more complicated and exclusive, such as, you can only play the game if you are wearing something blue, or if your name begins with J. You can also introduce handicaps, such as time limits or blindfolds.

Link in to the Bible study by pointing out how difficult the new rules made the game. The same sort of thing was happening in Colosse, where some teachers were introducing new rules for living as a Christian.

ACTIVITY

Photocopy page 48 for each group member. This puzzle is better done as a group activity. The verses used are Colossians 2:6-7.

There are no clues to the puzzle. First crack the code with the help of the given letters. Each small number refers to a specific letter. All the answers come from 2 verses in today's Bible passage. When you have completed the puzzle can you work out which 2 verses have been used?

Which Bible verses were used?

PREPARATION

Colossians 3:1-17

LESSON AIMS

To understand how a Christian should conduct himself in his relationship with Christ and with the local church.

Having explained what it means to be 'in Christ' (chs. 1-2), Paul now teaches how this should be worked out in daily life. It is impossible to **live** as a Christian without proper understanding of what it means to **be** a Christian. This lesson looks at the first 2 areas, the Christian's relationship with Christ and with the local church. The following lesson studies the Christian's relationships at home, at work and with the outsider.

Relationship with Christ

This relationship should be the chief priority for every Christian. It affects every other relationship.

3:1   The first thing Paul commands is to 'set your heart on things above'. Through Jesus Christ the Christian has constant access to the throne of God and is acceptable in his presence. The Christian's interests are to be focused on Christ.

3:2   The second command concerns the mind. The Christian must endeavour to get to know Christ, what he likes and what displeases him. These can be found by studying God's word. Setting the mind on things above does not mean being so heavenly minded that you are no earthly good. The earthly things are to do with those mentioned in v.5.

3:3   The old life has ended and a new one begun, so do not keep harking back to the old one. The Christian's life is 'hidden' in the sense that his union is with Christ in heaven, so is invisible to the world.

3:4   The new life in Christ will be fully evident only on Christ's return. It is only then that the blessings Christ gives will be fully present.

3:5   'Put to death' implies positive action on the part of the Christian. Paul is not talking about mortification of the body in an effort to repress sexuality, etc. These desires are normal and are found in every human heart. However, we must deal with them so that they do not mar

our testimony. The 5 sins listed are to do with licentiousness and avarice, both of which are very evident in present day society. The incentive to work hard at v.5 comes from both v.4 and v.6.

3:6   God is unalterably opposed to sin and will make sure that it is justly punished.

3:8   The 5 sins in this verse are all to do with behaviour (the 5 mentioned in v.5 are to do with the heart). The Christian is to rid himself of these in the same way as putting off dirty clothes. They are all sins of speech, associated with a pagan lifestyle, and make harmonious relationships impossible. 'Filthy' language can mean abusive language.

Relationship with the local church

3:9   This verse is also to do with speech and links the 2 sections. Truth between Christians must be paramount if the local church is to remain united. Unity is the theme running through these remaining verses.

3:10   Paul again points to the importance of the mind (v.2). The church is a new creation (see 2 Corinthians 5:17).

3:11   A barbarian was someone who did not speak Greek. Scythians were from Northern Greece and were considered to be uncouth by the Athenian Greeks. It is only when Christ is everything to every Christian that these barriers are broken down.

3:12   The language used of the church is the same God used for Israel (Exodus 19:5-6, Deuteronomy 7:6-8). The church is God's special possession, in the same way that Israel was in the OT, and should demonstrate the character of God if it is to take the gospel to the world. Note that effort is involved - clothes do not put themselves on!

3:14 Love is the final quality that will give 'perfect' unity. The new teachings would have caused disunity with their stress on the need for a new experience of God's power. Paul considered unity in the church to be vital. The local church then was just as full of problems as the church today!

3:15 Paul is not talking about an inner feeling of peace that demonstrates you are in God's will, but about harmony within the church. This bringing together of disparate units is a good reason for thankfulness, as it is impossible through human endeavour alone.

3:16 It is important to study the Bible because this is where Christ's word is found. The new teachers appear to have been basing their authority on God speaking to them through visions (2:18). Note that teaching and admonishing are to be done by **every** Christian, not just a special few. Differentiation can be made between psalms, hymns and spiritual songs, but does not affect the overall sense. Paul points out that their content should be consistent with Scripture.

3:17 The theme is still unity. Christ must be central to everything, to teaching (words), to plans and to activities (deeds).

1. Read verses 1-8. What practical things can you do to help you set your heart and mind on heavenly things? What does it mean, to put to death earthly things? What can help you do it?

2. We often find other Christians difficult to get on with. Why does Paul say unity is important among Christians? How can we help promote unity in the Christian groups we belong to? Is it ever right to separate from other Christians?

Get Rid of the Parcel! Prepare a parcel with 7 or 8 layers of wrapping and a bag of sweets or similar in the centre. For each layer of wrapping there needs to be a forfeit, which is acting out an activity in a particular style which needs to be 'put to death' from verses 5-14 in the Bible passage. Decide on the activity as a group, e.g. making a cup of tea, brushing your teeth, driving a car.

Sit the group members in a circle to play pass the parcel. Explain that they may not want to unwrap it. When the music stops the person holding the parcel unwraps one layer and looks at the forfeit. He/she performs the activity decided by the group at the start in the manner specified on the forfeit, e.g. angrily, proudly, greedily, impatiently, etc. The group has to guess which characteristic is being acted before the game continues. At the end screw up all the wrappings and throw them away.

Link in to the Bible study by pointing out how quickly the parcel was passed on by those who do not like acting and that the wrappings were thrown away at the end. Let's see what Paul says the Christians at Colosse should do with their old ways of behaviour.

Photocopy page 51 for each group member. The Bible verse is Colossians 3:2.

Find the following 17 words in the word square. Each word reads in a straight line horizontally, vertically or diagonally and can read backwards or forwards. No letter is used more than once.

D	S	E	T	Y	T	S	I	R	H	C	O
U	E	R	H	M	N	Y	D	E	A	T	H
I	H	S	N	U	T	A	D	S	E	O	N
T	E	H	I	I	M	I	T	G	N	W	G
S	A	A	N	A	B	I	D	U	I	O	F
D	R	U	D	V	R	E	L	S	R	O	E
E	T	N	N	E	L	G	D	I	R	E	P
W	S	O	E	W	T	O	L	G	T	T	E
E	O	N	O	S	M	A	I	O	E	Y	A
N	A	N	R	T	O	V	E	H	R	L	C
E	K	Y	T	H	E	H	I	S	N	Y	E
R	G	H	O	L	Y	S	C	E	V	O	L

CHOSEN
CHRIST
DEATH
FORGIVE
GLORY
HEARTS
HOLY
HUMILITY
KNOWLEDGE
LOVE
NATURE
PEACE
RAISED
RENEWED
SEATED
UNITY
WISDOM

Now, starting from the top and reading from left to right, write down the remaining letters to discover an important command.

Where does this verse come from?

PREPARATION
Colossians 3:18 - 4:18

LESSON AIMS
To learn how Christians should conduct themselves in the area of everyday relationships.

In verses 3:18 - 4:6 Paul continues his exposition on practical Christian living. These basic rules for family life were not made up by Paul, the Greeks already had firm ideas about right and proper behaviour. Paul gave them a new direction by pointing out that this area of life, like every other, should be lived under Christ's rule. There are three couplets with complementary responsibilities. In all three the subordinate party is addressed first. The gospel brought an equality and freedom that was not present in society. It was essential that this freedom was not misused so that the gospel was brought into disrepute. However, we should not dismiss Paul's teaching as being culturally determined and only for his own time. The reason for this behaviour is always to do with the Christian's relationship with Christ (3:18,20,22-23). Present day culture may be different but people's hearts are the same; in no culture have people enjoyed being submissive. It is important to keep each couplet together, because the 2 sides are mutually interdependent.

Relationships at home

3:18 The word used for submission describes the normal obligations for all citizens to lawful authority. It does not mean being reduced to menial service with no will or voice of your own. If the relationship called for it, as in the military, the term included obedience. In fact the word 'obey' does not appear in Scripture with respect to wives, though it does with respect to children obeying their parents (v.20) and slaves their masters (v.22). The reason given for this submission is because it is fitting in the Lord and is a natural outworking of life under Christ's rule. Submission has nothing to do with equality. Jesus is equal with God the Father, but is also subject to him (Philippians 2:6, 1 Corinthians 11:3; 15:28). The God-given chain of authority (1 Corinthians 11:3) is disregarded at our peril (witness what is happening in modern society). Submission is the duty of all believers one to the other (Ephesians 5:21).

3:19 This command was revolutionary in Paul's day, when wives were a possession. The word used for 'harsh' implies being embittered and critical. It is easier for a wife to submit to a loving husband and for a husband to love a loyal wife.

3:20 In this context obedience is a right demonstration of submissiveness. Note the balancing of 'in everything' with pleasing the Lord. Children are not being told to obey a parent who commands them to do something contrary to God's rule (e.g. steal). The home is where children learn respect for authority and this will stand them in good stead in later life, both in respect to submission to secular authorities and to God.

3:21 Note the command to fathers to cease from endless criticism and too harsh punishments. Again Paul points out the 2 sides to the relationship. It is easier for a child to obey a father who makes reasonable demands and for a father to govern an obedient child with a light hand.

Relationships at work

3:22-23 Paul makes no comment about the wrongs of slavery, rather he calls on slaves and masters to show Christian principles in their relationship with each other. He has already pointed out the equality of all believers in the sight of God (3:11) and is now concerned with how this equality works out in practice. The freedom experienced by the slave is freedom to do everything as work for Christ. He is called to offer real obedience, not just what is necessary to serve his own ends.

3:24-25 Work deserves to be rewarded - but so does shoddy service. God does not show favouritism, either for the rich or for the oppressed.

4:1   A slave had no recourse to justice, but this is what Paul is telling the master to give. Note the reason given for the master's compliance. Human relationships can only be put right if man's relationship with God is right.

Relationship with the outsider

4:2   In this next section Paul talks about the duty of the ordinary Christian to see that his neighbours hear about Christ. The first command is to pray (cf. 1:9; 4:12). 'Devote yourselves' implies perseverance.

4:3   This verse states that we should pray for all those, like Paul, called to the work of preaching and evangelism.

       The mystery of Christ - see 1:25-27.

4:4   Note that the gospel needs to be taught clearly, it is not 'caught' through friendship. Much is talked today of making relationships with children as a way of bringing them into relationship with Jesus. Unless there is **also** a clear proclamation of the gospel the second relationship will not occur. This is not to say that the first is unimportant!

4:5   The second command for the Christian is to do with conduct. The way we treat outsiders should demonstrate our new life in Christ.

4:5b-6 The third command is to make the most of every opportunity to answer the questions of our unbelieving neighbours/friends. Every Christian is called to do this, whereas every Christian is not called to preach. Note that our words should be gracious and seasoned with salt. Salt is a preservative and adds taste. Similarly the Christian conversation is to be good and wholesome, cf. Ephesians 4:29.

Concluding remarks

4:7-9 Paul sends news of his circumstances and reassures the Colossians that he knows about theirs (see also v.12).

       Tychicus was from Asia and accompanied Paul to Jerusalem (Acts 20:4). He also took Paul's letter to the Ephesians (Ephesians 6:21-22). He is also mentioned in 2 Timothy 4:12 and Titus 3:12.

       Onesimus was a converted runaway slave (see series overview).

4:10   Aristarchus was a Macedonian, who was with Paul during the Ephesian riot (Acts 19:29) and therefore known in Colosse. He

and Tychicus were with Paul in Greece (Acts 20:4), and he accompanied Paul on his trip to Rome (Acts 27:2).

Mark was the author of the gospel. Against Barnabas' advice Paul refused to take Mark on his 2nd missionary journey (Acts 15:38) but now, 12 years later, their earlier differences seem to have been overcome. In Paul's last letter, he even writes that Mark 'is helpful to me in my ministry' (2 Timothy 4:11).

4:12-13 Paul testifies that Epaphras has taught the Colossians properly and is concerned for their spiritual growth (see also 1:7).

4:14   Luke wrote about Paul in the book of Acts, having often been with him on his travels (Acts 16:10). He was with Paul in Rome during his imprisonment where this letter was written (Acts 28).

       Demas was a Christian worker who would later desert Paul (2 Timothy 4:10).

4:15   Nympha had a church in her house. There were no church buildings in those days.

4:16   Paul was concerned about what was happening in the churches as a result of the new teachings and wanted to make sure they understood the full gospel. Hence his insistence on their reading the letters. The letter from Laodicea does not mean a letter by the Laodiceans, but rather a Pauline letter to the Laodiceans which they then lent to the Colossians.

4:17   Archippus was part of the household of Philemon (Philemon v.2).

4:18   The apostle dictated his letter (see Romans 16:22) and at the end would himself write a few words of greeting. This would authenticate the letters.

1. What are the 3 pairs of relationships in 3:18 - 4:1? How should their behaviour complement each other?

2. Is it ever right for a child to disobey a parent (3:20-21)?

3. In 3:22 - 4:1 Paul talks about relationships at work. How do these instructions apply to the pupil/teacher relationship at school? (Think about use of time, resources, undermining authority, etc.)

4. How can we help ensure that the people we see every day hear about Jesus (4:2-6)?

Who Are You?   Cut out some pictures of famous people, such as pop stars, models, royalty, politicians, TV celebrities, from newspapers and magazines, or pictures of people with distinctive jobs, such as firefighters, doctors, nurses, police, chefs. On separate pieces of paper write descriptions of a typical day each cut-out person might have, who they might speak to, how they might do their job. Number the pictures and allocate a letter of the alphabet to each description. Pin up the pictures and descriptions around the walls. The aim of the game is to pair up the picture with the job description.

Link in to the Bible study by pointing out that people behave in a way that is appropriate to their job or role. How strange it would be to see a firefighter behaving like a nurse or a politician behaving like a pop star. Let's see what Paul has to say about the way Christians should behave.

Photocopy page 55 for each group member.

A Who's Who of Colossians

Can you unjumble the following list of names? All but one are people who have been mentioned in today's passage. The remaining one can be found at the beginning of the letter. If you need help there are a list of references at the bottom of the page.

Mased

Hiccyust

Ulke

Homitty

Happaser

Upla

Assurriatch

Eumisson

Manphy

Pushicarp

1. 4:14　　2. 4:7　　3. 4:14　　4. 1:1　　5. 4:12　　6. 4:18　　7. 4:10　　8. 4:9　　9. 4:15　　10. 4:17

OVERVIEW
Choose Life

SERIES AIMS

1. To teach the reality of a final judgment with only 2 destinations, heaven and hell.

2. To encourage the young people to tell their friends about Jesus.

MEMORY WORK

For the wages of sin is death, but the gift of God is eternal life in Christ Jesus our Lord.

Romans 6:23

Choose Life

This two week series follows on from the series, 'Is God Fair?', looking at predestination and what happens to those who have never heard the gospel (Book 3 weeks 18-19). We live in a pluralist society where political correctness states that all religions are equal and the doctrine of an eternal hell is deemed to be out-of-date. Many Christians have difficulties with the concept of eternal damnation, because real people come to mind. The concept of oblivion for those who do not acknowledge Jesus Christ as Lord is far more palatable, so it is important to look at the Bible to see what it really teaches. Also, we must be positive in our teaching and never teach about hell without reminding our young people about heaven. God has told us about hell to warn us, so that we have the opportunity to repent before it is too late.

The first lesson studies the Bible's teaching on hell and eternal judgment, looking at what hell is like, who will be there and what our response should be in the light of this teaching. The second lesson looks at who is acceptable to God and discusses the position of devout adherents of other religions. It is hoped that this series will spur the young people on to tell their non-Christian friends the good news of Jesus Christ.

PREPARATION

See lesson notes for relevant passages.

LESSON AIMS

To learn what the Bible says about hell and eternal judgment.

As with all the apologetics style lessons the teacher's preparation is crucial. These notes, and those for next week, are designed to give you some ideas about how to approach the subject. How exactly you teach the lesson is up to you. The larger and younger the class, the more structured the lesson will need to be. A book that is easy to read and gives a good overview of the Bible's teaching on hell and judgment is 'God, that's not fair!' by Dick Dowsett, published jointly by Overseas Missionary Fellowship and Send The Light.

Introduction
Start the lesson by asking the following questions:

1. What is the only certainty in your life and the lives of everyone on this planet? (Death - unless Jesus returns first.)

2. Does death worry you?

3. Have you been asked any of the following questions? Could you answer them?

   a) How can you believe in hell, fire and brimstone and eternal suffering? Surely death is like an endless sleep?

   b) Are you saying that I am going to hell?

   c) How can a God of love send anyone to hell?

Give each group member a piece of paper and give them a few minutes to state what they think hell is like, either in words or pictures. Discuss their descriptions. Link in to seeing how the Bible describes hell.

Divide the group into pairs and give each pair 2-3 passages to look up and report back to the group. Use a flip chart or similar to record their answers.

Is there a hell and what is it like?
Hell is a real place of final punishment. Jesus himself warned of hell (Matthew 5:22,29-30). The Bible refers to hell as a place of condemnation, torment, agony, suffering, fire and destruction.

Matthew 5:22	- a place of fire.
Matthew 5:29-30	- a place where the whole body can end up.

(The above 2 references come from the Sermon on the Mount, which most people agree is good!)

Matthew 10:28	- a place where soul and body will be destroyed.
Matthew 22:13	- a place of darkness and great grief.
Matthew 23:33	- a place of condemnation.
Mark 9:43	- a place where the fire never goes out.
Luke 16:22-26	- a place of torment and awareness.
John 3:36	- (by inference) a place where you are under God's wrath.
2 Thessalonians 1:9	- a place where you are shut out of God's presence.

It is certainly not a peaceful oblivion!

Is hell real or just symbolic?
The New Testament word for hell, 'Gehenna', comes from the Hebrew name of the valley of Hinnom. This was a valley just outside Jerusalem where children were sacrificed by fire to the god Molech (2 Kings 23:10, 2 Chronicles 28:3). In Jesus' time it was the rubbish dump and fires burnt there continuously. In later Jewish writings the name was used for the place where sinners were punished.

There must be some degree of symbolism in the language used to describe hell, as you cannot have total darkness where there is a continual fire. But, as all Scripture is inspired by God (2 Timothy 3:16), the symbolism must express the reality. We cannot get away from the fact that Jesus was talking about a real place.

Will hell go on for ever?

Some evangelical Christians believe that hell is not everlasting (annihalationism). This is because of the distress caused by the thought of people suffering eternally. The Bible, however, speaks of eternal divine retribution (Matthew 25:46, Hebrews 6:1-2, Jude:7).

Who will be there?

Will real people be in hell, or is it just for the devil and his angels? Some people quote the following texts as a proof of universal salvation.

John 12:32, 1 Timothy 4:10, 1 John 2:2

These texts do not teach the final salvation of everyone, but God's ability and willingness to save all who come to him in repentance and faith.

Those who will be in hell:

Matthew 13:40-42	- all who do evil.
Matthew 13:49-50	- the wicked.
Matthew 7:22-23	- those whom Jesus does not know.
Matthew 7:13-14	- it will not be just a few people.

Who decides which people go to hell?

We are not the Judge, we do not know other's hearts, but we must warn people that there is a Judge.

Hebrews 9:27	- judgment is inescapable.
Genesis 18:25	- God can be trusted to judge rightly.
John 5:24-30	- God the Father has given Jesus the authority to judge.
Acts 17:31	- Christ's judgment is just.

How can a God of love send people to hell?

God is holy and hates sin - he cannot change. We have all sinned and deserve to die. Because of God's great love for us he took our punishment on the cross, so that none of us need suffer. Our part is to believe and obey.

Romans 3:23, Romans 6:23, Romans 5:8, John 3:16

Our response

There are 2 questions that need answering as a result of this lesson:

1. Have I made sure of my final destination?

2. What am I doing about family and friends who are not Christian? (This will be looked at in greater detail in the next lesson, 'More Than One Way to God?')

PREPARATION

See lesson notes
for relevant
passages.

LESSON AIMS

To understand that
Jesus is the only
way to God.

In the previous lesson we looked at the reality of hell as a final destination for those who do not know God. This week we will discover who is included in that category.

Introduction
Use the focus activity to lead into the lesson.

Start the Bible study with a brief recapitulation of what was learnt last time. Then ask if any of them have ever been asked the following questions:

1. Surely the devout Muslim/Hindu/Jew is acceptable to God?

2. How can God condemn people for rejecting the Saviour of whom they've never heard?

3. What about babies who die?

Could they answer them?

What about the devout Muslim, etc?
Sincerity is not enough. One may be sincerely wrong. If other religions were acceptable to God then there was no need for Christ to suffer and die.

All religions recognise that man cannot approach God without earning the right to do so. The sacrifice offered could be behaviour/deeds, e.g. the pillars of Islam, gifts, penance, animal sacrifices, good living and reincarnations to reach the perfect state in Hinduism. The major world religions are very ethical, e.g. a devout Buddhist does not take life, does not steal, does not indulge in sexual immorality, does not lie and does not get drunk.

The world religions demonstrate the different ways man uses to approach God. We live in a pluralist society and are influenced by that society's thought forms. Things are deemed 'right' if they work. No longer are there absolutes of right and wrong. In the Bible, God's revelation to man, we discover that worship acceptable to God was not something people decided to do for God, but was following the instructions God had given

them. In Genesis 4:1-7 Cain and Abel both brought sacrifices to God. Abel's sacrifice was acceptable, but Cain's was not - he did not do what was right (v.7). The important question is how can sinful man be made right with a holy God?

Hebrews 9:22	forgiveness is only obtained through shedding of blood.
1 John 2:2	Jesus is the sacrifice for everyone's sins.
John 14:6	Jesus is the only way to God.
1 Timothy 2:5-6	there is only one mediator between God and man.

Unlike in man-made religions, Jesus is a mediator who is both God and man, therefore he is unique in his ability to unite man with God.

What about those who have never heard?
In the Old Testament godly people were saved by faith, even though they had never heard the gospel of Christ! They were saved through Jesus' death on the cross, just as we are (Hebrews 10:12). Could it not be that devout people of other religions are seeking after God and so will be acceptable to him on the basis of Christ's death, even though they are not 'Christian'?

| Acts 10:34-35 | These verses might appear to support the above argument. However, Peter is not suddenly realising that people of other religions who do right are acceptable to God, rather that God will accept non-Jews who come to him in repentance and faith. If Cornelius being devout and seeking after God was sufficient, God would not have needed to send Peter to tell him the gospel. |
| Acts 17:30-31 | We are not living in times past, so ignorance will not be overlooked. |

59

Is God fair?

Romans 2:1-16

The 3 principles by which God judges:

a) our own standards (v.1-4). Every time we criticise someone we are saying they are doing wrong. We even fail by our own standards.

b) our deeds (v.5-11). God holds each one of us responsible for our actions.

c) according to the knowledge or light a person has (v.12-15). Our own consciences condemn us.

Romans 3:19

We fail on all 3 counts.

(For a fuller study on the above passages see Book 3 Week 19, 'What about those who have never heard?') Those who have never heard the gospel are not condemned because they have not heard, but because of their sin.

Our response

People are heading for eternity without Christ, in total separation from God. In love we must warn them of the danger ahead.

Matthew 28:19-20 The great commission.

How do we do it? - loving, respectful, gentle, caring.

- friendship, evangelism, urgency, responsibility.

Only One Way   Divide the group into teams. Each team requires a blindfold and a set of blown-up balloons, a different colour for each team. You need one balloon for each team member plus one rogue balloon per team, which is a different pattern or colour from all the team colours.

The teams start at one end of the room and the balloons are placed at the other end. The team members take it in turns to be blindfolded and crawl to the other end of the room, directed by their team members. Once they reach their team's balloons they burst one before taking off the blindfold and returning to base. The winning team is the one to burst the most of their own colour balloons.

Link in to the Bible study by pointing out the importance of following their team mates' instructions, if they were to find their way to the right balloon, and the consequences of getting it wrong (bursting the wrong balloon). Let's see what the Bible has to say about the right way to God.

OVERVIEW
The Kings

Week 17 | **Introduction**   *1 Samuel 8:1-22; 13:13-14; 2 Samuel 7:8-16, 1 Kings 2:1-4; 11:9-13*
a) To see that God's people should be different from the world around them.
b) To learn about the covenant God made with David and his descendants.

Week 18 | **The Division of the Kingdom**   *1 Kings 12:1-33; 13:33-34; 14:21-31*
To see how God's word to Jeroboam was fulfilled and the devastating consequences of disobedience.

Week 19 | **Ahab**   *1 Kings 16:29-33; 21:1-29*
To learn that evil will be punished eventually.

Week 20 | **Jehoshophat**   *2 Chronicles 18:1 - 19:11*
To teach the foolishness of making alliances with God's enemies.

Week 21 | **Joash**   *2 Chronicles 22:10 - 24:27*
To teach the importance of being guided by godly people.

Week 22 | **Hezekiah**   *2 Kings 18:1 - 20:21*
To show the importance of trusting in God alone and not in our own strength.

Week 23 | **Manasseh**   *2 Chronicles 33:1-20*
To learn of God's mercy to repentant sinners.

Week 24 | **Josiah**   *2 Chronicles 34:1 - 35:27*
To teach the importance of obeying God's word.

Week 25 | **Into Exile**   *2 Chronicles 36:1-23, Jeremiah 39:1-10*
To see the outcome of persistent disobedience.

SERIES AIMS

1. To see God's plan for his people being worked out in the reigns of the kings.

2. To come to a deeper understanding of this period of Biblical history and how it fits into the whole picture of the Old Testament.

MEMORY WORK

If my people, who are called by my name, will humble themselves and pray
and seek my face and turn from their wicked ways, then will I hear from
heaven and will forgive their sin and will heal their land.
2 Chronicles 7:14

The Kings

The office of king was common in the Middle East from earliest times. The king was the ruler of a settled region, usually centred on a city (Genesis 14:1-2). Kings were normally, although not necessarily, hereditary and each king was thought to be descended from the god of that region. In Egypt Pharaoh was considered to be a manifestation of one of their gods, whereas in Assyria the king was only a representative of their god.

In early Israel the nomadic tribes were ruled by patriarchs, e.g. Abraham. During the Exodus Israel was ruled by Moses (Exodus 6:2-13), followed by Joshua (Deuteronomy 34:5-9) and then various judges (Judges 10:1-5), but for the whole of this part of their history the Israelites recognised God as their king. The book of Judges ends on a note of social chaos, which the people attributed to their lack of a king (Judges 21:25).

Some improvement in the social structure occurred with the advent of the Priest-Judges, Eli and Samuel. However, their sons, who were appointed by their fathers to succeed them as priests, were not God-fearing men (1 Samuel 2:12; 8:1-3). Israel was under constant harassment by the Philistines so the people went to Samuel to ask for a king. This displeased Samuel, because he saw it as a rejection of God as Israel's king (1 Samuel 8:6-9), but God told him to accede to the peoples' request and appoint Saul as the first king of Israel.

Saul had all the qualities required of a warrior king. He was tall, courageous, handsome and from a wealthy background. He started out well but eventually he was rejected by God because of his persistent disobedience (1 Samuel 15:10).

Saul was followed by David, who established a dynasty that was to last for 400 years. He was the ideal king, a man of action, a poet, generous in victory, a wise judge and loyal friend, but he too sinned against God (2 Samuel 11-12). The difference between David and Saul was shown by David's response when faced with his sin - repentance.

God forgave David but said that, as a result of his sin, in each succeeding generation some of David's descendants would die by violence and that David would be troubled by members of his own family (2 Samuel 12:10-12). This came to pass as God said, when first Absalom, then Adonijah, tried to take the throne from their father David (2 Samuel 13-19, 1 Kings 1-2).

David was succeeded by his son Solomon, who was the first dynastic king. He started out ruling wisely and well, but problems arose with the building of the temple, when Israelites were drafted in as forced labour (1 Kings 5:13-14). This, together with heavy taxation, was a direct fulfilment of Samuel's prophecy (1 Samuel 8:10-18) and led to the eventual revolt of the 10 northern tribes (1 Kings 12:4-16). Solomon's fatal flaw was disobedience. He married many wives, foreigners with their own pagan religions (1 Kings 11:1-2), and this led to syncretism. Punishment from God came in the form of various revolts (1 Kings 11:14-40) although, for David's sake, God did not depose him (1 Kings 11:34-35).

After Solomon's death he was succeeded by his son Rehoboam and shortly afterwards the 10 northern tribes (Israel) rebelled and made Jeroboam their king, leaving Rehoboam as king of Judah. Israel became quickly paganised and after several coups was eventually defeated by the Assyrians in 722 BC. The population was deported and the area occupied by people from other nations. Judah was less paganised but only preserved because of God's faithfulness to his promise to David (2 Samuel 7:12-17, 1 Kings 11:34-36). Eventually Judah was overrun by the Babylonians in 587 BC, Jerusalem was destroyed and the people were taken into exile.

This series deals with the division of the kingdom and events in the lives of 6 kings, 5 from Judah and one from Israel. For a list of the kings of Israel and Judah see pages 63.

Kings of Israel

God → Saul → David → Solomon → Division of the Kingdom

Judah		Israel	
King	**Years on throne**	**King**	**Years on throne**
Rehoboam	17	Jeroboam	22
Abijah	3		
Asa	41		
		Nadab	2
		Baasha	24
		Elah	2
		Zimri	7 days
		Omri	12
		Ahab	22
Jehoshaphat	25		
		Ahaziah	2
		Joram	12
Jehoram	8		
Ahaziah	1		
Queen Athaliah	6	Jehu	28
Joash	40		
		Jehoahaz	17
		Jehoash	16
Amaziah	29		
		Jeroboam II	41
Azariah	52		
		Zechariah	6 months
		Shallum	1 month
		Menahem	10
		Pekahiah	2
		Pekah	20
Jotham	16		
Ahaz	16		
		Hoshea	9
Hezekiah	29		
		Exile	
Manasseh	55		
Amon	2		
Josiah	31		
Jehoahaz	3 months		
Jehoiakim	11		
Jehoiachin	3 months		
Zedekiah	11		
Exile			

PREPARATION

1 Samuel 8:1-22; 13:13-14.
2 Samuel 7:8-16,
1Kings 2:1-4; 11:9-13

LESSON AIMS

a) To see that God's people should be different from the world around them.

b) To learn about the covenant God made with David and his descendants.

1 Samuel

8:4-5 Samuel was getting old, and the elders saw that there was no obvious successor to continue the fight against the Philistines. Samuel's sons were at Beersheba, far away to the south of Ramah, not under his direct supervision. With both Eli and Samuel, it became obvious that good men can have evil children (see 2:12).

Note the reason why the people wanted a king - to be like the other nations.

8:6-9 Asking for a king was rejecting God (their king). God told Samuel to do what the people wanted but to warn them of the consequences. The sin of Israel in requesting a king did not rest in any evil inherent in kingship, but rather in the kind of king they wanted, and their reasons for so doing. Their desire was for the kind of king that denied the special covenant relationship with the Lord, who himself had pledged to be their saviour and deliverer. They wanted a king like other nations (8:20), thus ignoring the covenant and forgetting that God had provided for and led them in the past.

8:10-17 Samuel warned the people what would happen when they were ruled by a human king.

8:18 By the time the people realise how foolish they have been in asking for a human king it will be too late - when they cry out to God for relief he will not hear them.

13:13-14 Samuel tells Saul 'you acted foolishly'. Saul's sin was that he thought he could strengthen Israel's chances against the Philistines while disregarding the Lord's instructions given through his prophet, Samuel.

2 Samuel

7:8-16 In these verses, through the prophet Nathan, God promises David that his line will continue for ever and that his son will build the temple.

7:10-11 When ruled by a good king, God's people will have security in the land God has given them.

The house referred to here is the Davidic dynasty.

7:14 This verse states that some of David's descendants would be bad kings and would receive divine punishment.

7:16 In 587 BC the temple was destroyed and Judah ceased to be a kingdom. Although the family of David continued to exist they never regained the throne. This verse points forward to the coming of the Lord Jesus, 'great David's greater Son'.

1 Kings

2:1-4 Before dying, David charges his son Solomon to be strong and to obey God. He will then prosper in all his works and wherever he goes. David remembers God's promise to him, that if his descendants are faithful to God in their hearts and souls they will always have a king on the throne of David.

11:9-13 Here God speaks to Solomon, David's son, for the final time. Solomon had broken the covenant (see verses 1-8) despite every blessing he had received from God's hand, but, for David's sake, disaster would be postponed until the reign of Solomon's successor, and when it came it would not deprive him of the whole kingdom.

QUESTIONS

1. Israel wanted a king, in order to be like other nations. Why was this wrong? Discuss the ways the church, (the new Israel), should be different from the world around.

2. Look at the promise God made to David in 2 Samuel 7:8-16 and compare it with David's charge to Solomon in 1 Kings 2:1-4. How did Solomon go wrong? What can we learn from this to help us in our Christian life?

FOCUS ACTIVITY

Peer Pressure Divide the young people into groups of 3 or 4 and give each group a few magazines and a pair of scissors. Ask them to cut out pictures or adverts depicting items they would like to have. Display the cut-outs and discuss what makes these items desirable. Lead the discussion into the area of peer pressure and how this affects their lives. Link in to the Bible study by pointing out that peer pressure affects everyone, even people your age! Let's see what happened to God's people when they decided they wanted to be like everyone else.

ACTIVITY

On page 66 is a time chart of the rise and fall of a nation, which is best done as a group exercise. On a flip chart draw a line down the page and write in the dates and headings as per the time chart. Fill in the country, events and people as a group. This exercise will help the group locate the kings at the correct point in Israel's history. Page 66 can be photocopied for each group member to take home.

The Rise and Fall of a Nation

Country	BC	Events	People
		Creation	Adam & Eve
		The Fall	
		The Flood	Noah
		The Tower of Babel	
Canaan	c.2000	The rise of the Patriarchs	Abraham
			Isaac
			Jacob
Egypt	c.1700	Jacob's family settle in Egypt	Joseph
Egypt	c.1500	Slavery in Egypt	
Wilderness	c.1300	Rescue from Egypt	Moses
Canaan	c.1250	Entry into Canaan	
		The time of the Judges	Joshua
			Gideon
			Samson
			Ruth
			Samuel
Israel	c.1050	The start of the Monarchy	Saul
			David
			Solomon
Israel & Judah	931	The division of the kingdom	
Judah	722	Israel taken into exile	
	587	Destruction of Jerusalem Judah taken into exile	

PREPARATION

1 Kings 12:1-33;
13:33-34; 14:21-31

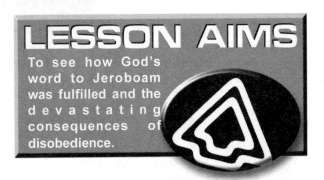

LESSON AIMS

To see how God's word to Jeroboam was fulfilled and the devastating consequences of disobedience.

12:1 Shechem was an important city in the hill country of Ephraim. It was where God appeared to Abraham and repeated his promise about the land (Genesis 12:6-7), and where Joshua called the people together for a renewal of the covenant (Joshua 24).

12:2 Jeroboam was an able leader entrusted by Solomon with the entire labour force of the northern tribes (see 11:26-28). It is not stated why Solomon tried to kill Jeroboam (11:40). It may be that Solomon had heard about Ahijah's prophecy.

12:4 The people express grave discontent with Solomon's heavy taxation and conscripted labour (see 4:27-28; 5:13-14).

12:7 The proper role of the king was a servant to his people.

12:8 The men were young in comparison with the men who had served Solomon. Rehoboam was 41 years old when he became king. By listening to his contemporaries and turning his back on the men who had advised his father, Rehoboam is demonstrating his stupidity.

12:15 See 1 Kings 11:29-37. Human beings have freedom to obey or disobey, but this freedom is contained within God's sovereignty.

12:18 Adoniram - see 4:6; 5:14.

12:25 Jeroboam established his kingdom in two ways, firstly by strengthening the 2 key cities of Shechem and Peniel.

12:26-28 Secondly, Jeroboam reorganised the worship of Israel (the 10 northern tribes now under

his rule). He created 2 cultic centres at Dan and Bethel (v.29). Note that this was sold to the people as something to make life easier for them (v.28). They were still worshipping the same God, just in a different place! Jeroboam's fear shows his lack of trust in the promises God had given him through Ahijah that, if he remained obedient, God would establish for him an everlasting dynasty (11:37-39).

12:28-31 The golden calves led people into idolatry. Jeroboam further compounded his sin by setting up lesser shrines in high places, and staffing them with illegitimate priests.

13:32-34 Jeroboam's persistent sin led to Israel's total destruction later. Note the introduction of a man-made festival. The Jewish festivals had all been instituted by God (cf. Leviticus 23:1-44).

14:21 Rehoboam's mother was an Ammonite. Solomon's sin was marrying foreign wives, who led him to follow foreign gods (see 11:1-6).

14:22-24 The religious practices in Judah were every bit as bad as those in Israel. However, Rehoboam was not condemned for being personally involved, unlike Jeroboam (13:33-34).

14:25-26 By mentioning the Egyptian invasion at this point the author is implying that it was a divine punishment (cf. Judges 2:10-15).

14:27 Bronze shields replaced gold ones. The reduced fortunes of Rehoboam meant he could not match the wealth of Solomon, his father.

Summary

After Solomon's death his son, Rehoboam, succeeded him as king. The 10 northern tribes rebelled and made Jeroboam their king. The northern tribes were called Israel and the 2 southern tribes, Judah. The Israelites under Jeroboam were led into idolatry and evil practices, which would lead to eventual punishment from God. Rehoboam retained control of the southern kingdom of Judah, with Jerusalem its capital, but like the northern kingdom Judah soon adopted evil practices.

The book of Kings traces the fortunes of both these kingdoms to their end in exile.

1. How did Jeroboam's lack of trust in God's promises lead him astray?

2. Rehoboam asked advice of two groups of people, but heeded the wrong ones. Whose advice should we seek, and should we always obey it?

A map to show the division of the kingdom (see page 69).

Consequences Sit the group members in a circle facing inwards and give each one a number. Explain the following rules of the game and state that every time a rule is broken that player will be marked on the forehead with a spot of lipstick.

1. On their turn each player calls out their number, followed by the phrase 'no pink spots', followed by another person's number.
2. Play passes to the person whose number is called out second
3. No- one is allowed to repeat the number of the person who numbered them.
4. Any player with one or more pink spots on their forehead must change the middle phrase from 'no pink spots' to the number of spots on their forehead, e.g. 'one pink spot', 'two pink spots' etc.
5. Play should pass quickly from one person to another and pink spots are awarded for any delay or mistake.

The leader designates one person to start.

Link in to the Bible study by pointing out that breaking the rules of the game had consequences. The game had funny consequences, but the consequences of breaking God's rules are far more serious, as we shall see in today's Bible study.

Act out the confrontation of Jeroboam and Rehoboam. Split the group in half and ask them to prepare a play to act to each other. The play can be either the Bible story or a modern adaptation, e.g. a television news report from our man at Shechem. Each group is responsible for organising themselves. They should appoint a director, who can then decide with his/her group on the script, apportion parts, etc.

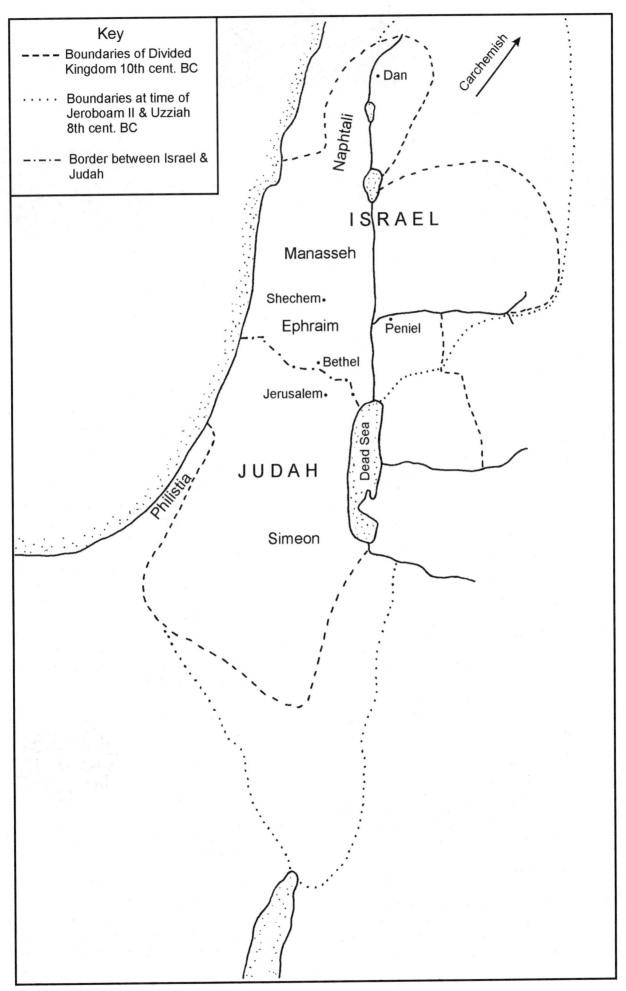

Key

- – – – Boundaries of Divided Kingdom 10th cent. BC
- · · · · Boundaries at time of Jeroboam II & Uzziah 8th cent. BC
- –·–·– Border between Israel & Judah

Carchemish

Dan

Naphtali

ISRAEL

Manasseh

Shechem·

Ephraim

·Peniel

·Bethel

Jerusalem·

Dead Sea

JUDAH

Philistia

Simeon

PREPARATION

1 Kings 16:29-33;
21:1-29

LESSON AIMS

To learn that evil
will be punished
eventually.

Between Jeroboam and Ahab there had been 5 other Kings of Israel (see page 63). During those reigns evil had progressively increased. Nearly one third of the narrative in 1 and 2 Kings concerns the 34 year period covering the reigns of Ahab and his 2 sons, Ahaziah and Joram. During this time there was a heightening of the struggle between God's kingdom (championed by Elijah and Elisha) and Satan's.

16:30   Note how Ahab is introduced.

16:31   Ahab married Jezebel and this allied him with Tyre and Sidon. During Ahab's reign religious life in Israel reached an all-time low. Ahab and Jezebel introduced the worship of the Phoenician god, Baal-melqart, who was worshipped as a weather god. Jezebel was also responsible for the persecution of worshippers of Yahweh (1 Kings 18:4).

16:32   Ahab not only set up altars to foreign gods, but also built a temple for Baal in Samaria.

21:1   Ahab had a second palace at Jezreel, in addition to the one in Samaria, which was the capital of the Northern Kingdom.

21:2   Ahab's request seems reasonable to modern readers, who buy and sell land as it suits.

21:3   However, as an Israelite, Ahab knew that Naboth had a religious duty, according to the law, regarding his land (Numbers 36:7, Leviticus 25:23). Naboth was right to say no because land was recognised to be a gift of God. By selling his land Naboth would be rejecting God's gift.

21:4   Ahab acted like a spoilt child.

21:7   An Israelite king was bound by the covenant law of Yahweh just as were his subjects. Jezebel could not understand this view, coming from her despotic background.

21:8-10   Jezebel arranged Naboth's death through a contrived situation which followed the letter of the Deuteronomic law (Leviticus 24:15-16; Deuteronomy 19:15).

21:13   2 Kings 9:26 states that Naboth's sons were put to death as well.

21:15-16   Jezebel masterminded each step of the plot.

21:19   Ahab had willingly gone along with his wife's schemes, making him guilty of murder and theft.

     Ahab's subsequent repentance postponed the fulfilment of this prophecy (see v.28-29). Ahab later died in battle and his body was brought back to Samaria and buried. The dogs licked the blood washed from his chariot (22:34-38). His son, Joram, was killed by Jehu and thrown onto the field of Naboth (2 Kings 9:23-26). Jezebel's death is recorded in 2 Kings 9:30-37.

21:27   Surprisingly, Ahab repented and God's judgment was postponed for one more generation (v.28-29).

QUESTIONS

1. Which of the 10 commandments had Ahab broken? What does this show about the possible consequences of sin?

2. Ahab repented of his sin and judgment was averted. How does this tie in with God's word to Elijah in 21:17-19? What does this passage teach about punishment for sin? How does this help in situations where people appear to get away with wrongdoing?

Getting Away With It! Stand in a circle with everyone facing inwards. Designate someone to start. The first player performs a simple action, such as clapping hands or standing on one foot. Play passes to the left and that person repeats the first action and adds a second action. Play passes clockwise around the circle with each player adding an action having repeated all the previous actions. Any player who makes a mistake is awarded a point. That player starts the game again with a single action and play passes clockwise around the circle. At the end tot up the points to determine winners and losers (the people with the most points).

Link in to the Bible study by pointing out that those people who got it wrong appeared to be getting away with it during the game. In real life we see people ignoring God and his laws and not seeming to suffer for it. Let's see what the Bible has to say about those people.

Photocopy page 72 for each group member. The word is 'repented'.

Write the words of the Bible verse below into the grid. The word 'I' is not included. When you have finished, take the letters from the shaded squares and rearrange them to see what Ahab did when confronted with his sin.

If my people, who are called by my name, will humble themselves and pray and seek my face and turn from their wicked ways, then will I hear from heaven and will forgive their sin and will heal their land.

(2 Chronicles 7:14)

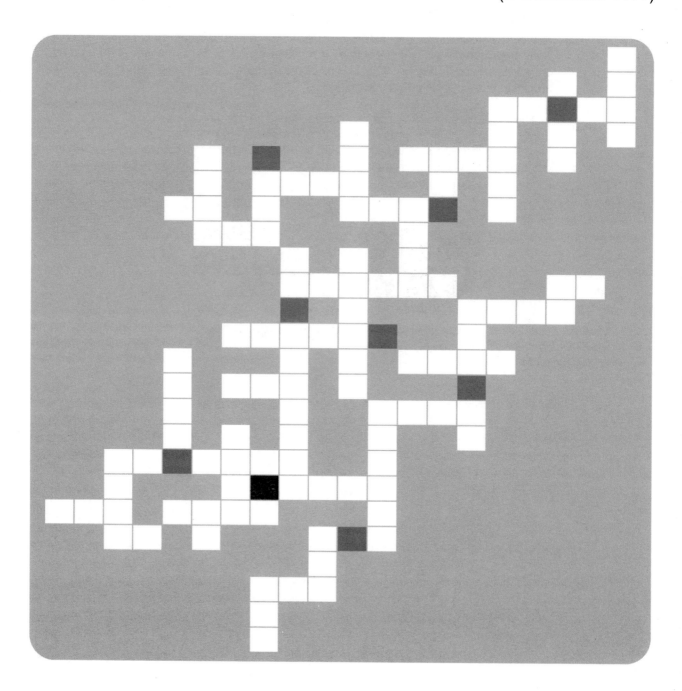

Ahab _ _ _ _ _ _ _ _

PREPARATION

2 Chronicles 18:1 - 19:11

LESSON AIMS

To teach the foolishness of making alliances with God's enemies.

1 and 2 Chronicles were written following the Jews' return from exile in Babylon. They look back on the history of Israel prior to the division of the kingdom, and Judah following it, and were written as an encouragement and to teach important lessons.

Jehoshaphat was the 4th king of Judah and reigned in Jerusalem c. 873-849 BC. He strengthened Judah against aggression from Israel by fortifying garrisons in the northern towns (2 Chronicles 17:2,12-13). Jehoshaphat was concerned to obey God's word, so he not only destroyed the pagan places of worship, but also provided itinerant teachers to teach it to the people (17:7-9). As a result the surrounding lands came to fear the God of Judah and so the land was at peace (17:10-11). The mistake Jehoshaphat made was in entering into an alliance with Ahab, king of Israel, by taking Ahab's daughter Athaliah as wife for his son Jehoram (18:1).

18:1   This kind of alliance was a common way of obtaining peace between countries. However, Jehoshaphat did not need this alliance (17:10) and was later rebuked for it (19:2).

18:2   Jehoshaphat's status is shown by noting the large number of animals slaughtered in his honour.

Ramoth Gilead was one of the Cities of Refuge for the tribe of Gad (Joshua 21:38) and had been captured by the Syrians.

18:3   Military alliance with Ahab was as ill-advised as a marriage. Here is a king, who starts well (chapter 17), falling into the trap of following human wisdom (chapter 18), a similar pattern to that of his father Asa.

18:4   It was common practice to consult God before going into battle.

18:6   This verse implies that Jehoshaphat recognised that the 400 prophets were not speaking the truth.

18:15   Ahab recognised that Micaiah was not speaking the truth.

18:19-21   The 'lying spirit' - some people have difficulty in accepting that God can send deceiving and evil spirits, but this is consistent with other passages of Scripture (cf. 1 Samuel 16:14-23, Job 1:12; 2:1-6). God is in control of everything, and that includes Satan. However, man still has the power to choose which way he will go. Jehoshaphat and Ahab are given the choice - and choose wrongly.

18:29   Ahab sought to avert possible disaster (18:22) by disguising himself and setting up Jehoshaphat in his place. This demonstrates Ahab's dominant position in the alliance.

18:31   Jehoshaphat was rescued through God's intervention.

18:33-34   Ahab was killed 'by chance'. He could not hide from God!

19:1   Jehoshaphat returned safely to Jerusalem - Micaiah's words were fulfilled (18:16).

19:4-11   Jehoshaphat means 'the Lord judges', which is an appropriate name for a king who instituted legal reform. These new arrangements would be of particular interest to the Chronicler, who was writing in the post-exilic period when their court would have been conducted along the lines of Jehoshaphat's reforms.

19:8   Traditionally justice was administered by the city elders, now the priests were also involved.

QUESTIONS

1. Why does the Bible record the bad as well as the good deeds of Jehoshaphat? How is this helpful for us?

2. Why do you think Jehoshaphat allied himself with Ahab? What does that teach us about trusting in God?

3. Does this passage teach that we should have no dealings with non-Christians? How can we discern when a relationship has become an alliance?

FOCUS ACTIVITY

Find Your Friends Prior to the meeting write down a number of well-known nursery rhymes on strips of paper, one line per strip. You require sufficient nursery rhymes to provide one strip for each group member. Scatter the strips on the floor in the middle of the room. On the given signal the young people grab a strip of paper and look for the group members who have the strips needed to complete the nursery rhyme. The winners are the first group to find each other and recite their nursery rhyme out loud.

Link in to the Bible study by pointing out the necessity of joining with the right people to complete the task. Let's see what the Bible has to say about making alliances with the wrong people.

ACTIVITY

Photocopy page 75 for each group member. The person left out of the puzzle is Amariah the chief priest (19:11).

By tracing a continuous path up, down and across through the word square can you find 16 names mentioned in the Bible passage? There are 2 kings, 1 prince, 3 prophets, 2 leaders, 3 countries and 5 places.

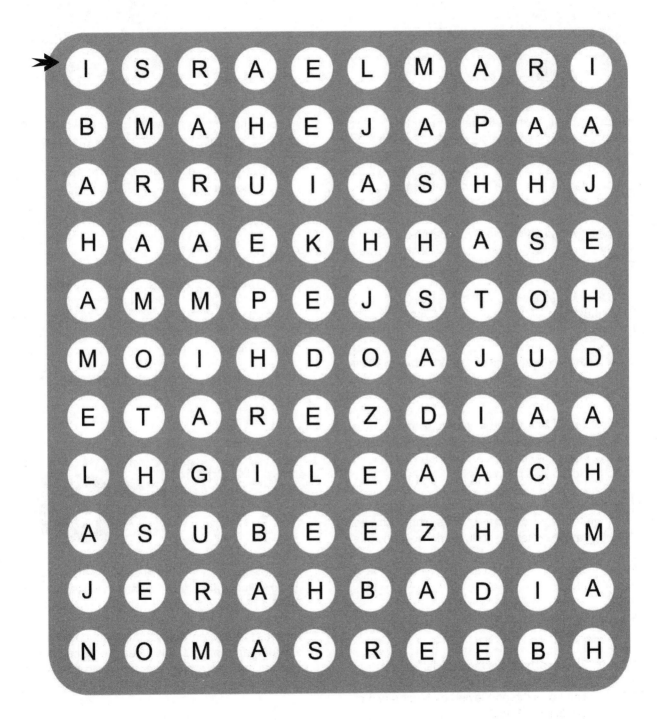

I	S	R	A	E	L	M	A	R	I
B	M	A	H	E	J	A	P	A	A
A	R	R	U	I	A	S	H	H	J
H	A	A	E	K	H	H	A	S	E
A	M	M	P	E	J	S	T	O	H
M	O	I	H	D	O	A	J	U	D
E	T	A	R	E	Z	D	I	A	A
L	H	G	I	L	E	A	A	C	H
A	S	U	B	E	E	Z	H	I	M
J	E	R	A	H	B	A	D	I	A
N	O	M	A	S	R	E	E	B	H

Read 19:8-11. What is the name and occupation of the person left out of the puzzle?

PREPARATION

2 Chronicles
22:10 - 24:27

LESSON AIMS

To teach the importance of being guided by godly people.

Jehoshaphat had been succeeded by his son Jehoram, who was married to Athaliah, daughter of Ahab. This alliance proved to be very ill-judged and wrong. Jehoram killed off all his brothers in order to secure his position (21:4). He reigned for 8 years, eventually dying from an incurable bowel disease, to no-one's regret (21:18-20). Jehoram was succeeded by his son, Ahaziah, who also 'walked in the ways of Ahab', encouraged by his mother, Athaliah (22:2-4). Ahaziah reigned for 1 year and was killed by Jehu, son of Nimshi, whom God had appointed to destroy the house of Ahab (22:7).

This is a long passage so it may be wise to read 22:10-12 with the group, paraphrase 23:1-21 and read 24:1-27.

23:1-3   Jehoiada acts. He makes an agreement with all the influential people in Judah to place the rightful king on the throne.

23:11   Joash is crowned king and given a copy of the covenant (contract), which the people had made with him in 23:3. Joash was 7 years old (cf. 24:1).

23:16   The relationship of the king and people with God was reaffirmed. This whole chapter demonstrates the godly wisdom of Jehoiada.

24:1   Joash's mother was from Beersheba in Judah.

24:2   Note the good influence Jehoiada had on Joash.

24:3   The royal house is re-established.

24:5   The tax is the one levied by Moses (v.6 cf. Exodus 30:11-16).

24:10   Note the joyful giving of the people.

24:15-16   Jehoiada's burial with the kings was a sign of the respect in which he was held, in contrast to 24:25, where Joash was not buried with the kings because of his great wickedness.

24:17   The officials mentioned here may have been followers of Athaliah. Joash comes over as being easily influenced.

24:19   The prophets were sent to cause the people to turn back to God, but they would not listen. Judah's failure to listen to the Lord's prophets ultimately led to her destruction (see 36:16).

24:26   Ammon and Moab were traditional enemies of Israel.

QUESTIONS

1. Contrast Joash under the influence of Jehoiada with Joash without Jehoiada. What can we learn from this?

2. Discuss the different things that influence our lives, for good and for bad. How can we discern what sort of influence a thing/relationship will have on us?

FOCUS ACTIVITY

Influences Hand out a piece of paper to each group member and give them 2 minutes to write down the categories of people who most influence them, such as parents, teachers, friends, celebrities, etc. Either collect in the papers and read out what has been said or ask the group to read out their answers. Record the answers on a flipchart. Discuss who influences them and how.

Link in to the Bible study by pointing out the importance of being influenced by the right people. In today's Bible study we will see who influenced King Joash and what happened as a result.

ACTIVITY

Photocopy page 78 for each group member. The question is, 'Who influences you?'

With the help of the clues on the right, add one letter to each of the words on the left to make a new word. Write the new letter in the box provided. Then unscramble the letters in the boxes and write them in the spaces below to find an important question. Two letters have been filled in to start you off.

Word	Box	Clue
FAT		not a theory
BIGHT		mildew
AIL		frozen rain
SPRIG		jump
AS		past tense of is
POT		sulk
PAT		gone by
BUT		trial of strength
DID		Jesus did this so that we can live
HAVE		a safe place
GOD		what God said about creation
EAR		12 months
RAN		Noah had this for 40 days and 40 nights
LED		ran away
PROD		a characteristic of some Pharisees
CRATED		what God did in the beginning

W _ _   _ _ _ _ _ _ _ _ _ _ _   Y _ _ ?

78

PREPARATION

2 Kings 18:1 - 20:21

LESSON AIMS

To show the importance of trusting in God alone and not in our own strength.

Following the death of Joash, his son Amaziah succeeded him as king. He is recorded as doing 'what was right in the eyes of the LORD, but not wholeheartedly' (2 Chronicles 25:2). Like his father, Amaziah started well, but finished badly. He was succeeded by his son, Uzziah, who 'did what was right in the eyes of the LORD, just as his father Amaziah had done' (2 Chronicles 26:4). God blessed Uzziah and he became powerful, but his pride led to his downfall. He attempted to burn incense in the temple, which was against God's law, and was struck down with leprosy (2 Chronicles 26:16-21). Uzziah was succeeded by his son, Jotham, who was another good king (2 Chronicles 27:2). He, in turn, was succeeded by his son, Ahaz, who followed the ways of the kings of Israel and reinstituted Baal worship (2 Chronicles 28:1-4). In Ahaz' time Judah was defeated by the Syrians and the Israelites and suffered many casualties. Ahaz called on Assyria for help and plundered the temple to provide tribute for the Assyrian king (28:16,21). He shut up the temple and encouraged the people to turn away from God (28:22-24).

This is a long passage and parts may need to be paraphrased.

18:1   Hoshea became king of Israel in the 12th year of Ahaz' reign. He was the last king of Israel, reigning for 9 years. He was defeated by the Assyrians and his people were taken into exile (2 Kings 17:1-6).

18:3   Hezekiah was one of the few kings who is compared favourably with David.

18:4   The bronze snake (Numbers 21:8-9) had not started out as an idol, but over the centuries, as the Israelites left off serving God, idolising the snake had crept into their religious practices.

18:7   Judah had become a vassal of Assyria under Ahaz (16:7).

18:8   At this time the Philistines were subject to Assyria.

18:9-11   Israel was taken into captivity in 722 BC, in the 6th year of Hezekiah's reign.

18:13   Sennacherib, king of Assyria, invaded Judah in 701 BC, in the 14th year of Hezekiah's reign. It is thought that there was a period of time when Hezekiah and Ahaz reigned together and the dating of the invasion of Judah is 14 years since Hezekiah took over as sole ruler.

18:14   The Assyrian records of the time note the tribute paid by Hezekiah, but increase the amount.

18:15-16   Note that Hezekiah used the silver from the temple as well as that from the royal treasuries.

18:17   In spite of the payment Sennacherib sends his army against Jerusalem.

18:19-25   The commander's speech is all to do with where the people of Jerusalem put their trust. There are 4 lines of argument:-

a)   There is no point in depending on Egypt, because it is too weak (v.21).

b)   There is no point in depending on God, because Hezekiah has taken down all the high places where he was worshipped (v.22).

c)   There is no point in depending on their army, because Judah's army is so depleted that even if Sennacherib provided the horses, Hezekiah could not put riders on them (v.23-24).

d)   The Lord himself has told the Assyrians to attack (v.25).

18:26   Aramaic was the international language of the Near East. What is surprising is that the 3 officials were able to speak in the dialect of the common people of Judah.

18:27   The commander gives a graphic picture of the outcome of a siege.

18:29   'This is what the king says ...' - the Assyrians now address their remarks to the people directly, rather than to Hezekiah's officials.

18:31-32 A time of peace and prosperity is promised for those who surrender to the Assyrians.

18:33-35 The commander puts God on a level with other gods and boasts that God cannot save his people.

18:37   Torn clothes was a sign of great grief.

19:1-2   Hezekiah's reaction in putting on sackcloth is a sign of mourning. He then sends to Isaiah.

19:4   One of the jobs of the prophets was to intercede with God on behalf of the people. Perhaps this is why the officials speak of God as 'your God' rather than 'our God'.

         The remnant is the people of Jerusalem. Many of the towns of Judah have already fallen to Sennacherib (see Isaiah 1:7-9).

19:7   This prophecy was fulfilled (see 19:35-37).

19:8-9   Things start to happen just as Isaiah said.

19:15   Hezekiah's prayer begins with an acknowledgement of God's greatness and sovereignty.

19:19   The purpose of Hezekiah's prayer is to ask God to demonstrate that he is sovereign.

19:21-28 Isaiah pronounces God's judgment on the Assyrians because of their arrogance and blasphemy.

19:32   Sennacherib was by then at Libnah and would not be able to carry out his threat against Jerusalem.

19:36   Nineveh was the capital of the Assyrian empire.

20:1   'In those days' suggests that this event happened round about the same time as the events of chapter 19. In 20:6 God promises Hezekiah a further 15 years of life, which would date the illness as occurring in

Hezekiah's 14th year as king, i.e. the year of Sennacherib's invasion (18:13). Also v.6 speaks of the future deliverance of Jerusalem, which suggests that this happened whilst Jerusalem was under siege. The reason the events are not in chronological order may be because the incidents recorded in chapter 20 do not show Hezekiah in a favourable light, so are placed here as a contrast to the previous chapters. They also act as a way into the story of Manasseh, who succeeded his father Hezekiah and who was one of the worst kings in Judah's history.

20:2-3   Note Hezekiah's reaction to the news of his own death.

20:7   This treatment was fairly typical of medical practice in those days. It was effective because of God's promise.

20:8-11 Hezekiah demonstrates no trust in God on this occasion. He chooses the more difficult of the signs and God, in his graciousness, grants his request.

20:12-21 This incident demonstrates Hezekiah's foolishness.

         Merodach-Baladan ruled in Babylon in 721-710 BC before being made to submit to Assyrian domination by Sargon II of Assyria. He may have sent Hezekiah gifts and letters to draw him into an alliance against Assyria.

20:13   Hezekiah's reception of the envoys was excessive. Perhaps he was attempting to bolster Judah's security by impressing the Babylonians with his power and wealth, but this was false security, as his trust should have been in God and not in reliance on foreign powers.

20:17   This is a prediction of the Babylonian exile at least 115 years before it happened. This was all the more remarkable in that, when Isaiah spoke, it was Assyria rather than Babylon who was the major power in that part of the world.

20:19   Note Hezekiah's self-centred response.

20:21   Manasseh was born during Hezekiah's extra 15 years of life (see 21:1).

1. List Hezekiah's good and bad points. Hezekiah means 'Yahweh is (my) strength'. In what ways did he prove true to his name?

2. Look at 18:19-35. What made the commander's speech likely to persuade the people to surrender?

3. In what ways are we tempted to trust in our own strength rather than in God?

FOCUS ACTIVITY

Strong Man   Fill 2 bags or crates with books. They should weigh the same and able to be lifted by one person with difficulty or 2 people more easily. Ask for volunteers who think they are strong to form a team to race against the rest. Form a second team of the same number of pairs as volunteers. Half of each team starts at one end of the room and half at the other end. Run a relay race, transporting the bags of books backwards and forwards across the room. The winning team is the first one to finish (should be the team of pairs).

Link in to the Bible study by pointing out that the team relying on their own strength lost out, whereas the one using help won. Let's look at the Bible to see if King Hezekiah relied on God or on himself.

ACTIVITY

Quiz
Split the group into 2 teams. The winner is the first team to collect 6 green vine leaves to place on their stem.

Requirements
Each team requires a drawing of a brown stem and a set of 8 vine leaves (see diagram). 6 vine leaves are coloured green and 2 brown. The leaves are randomly numbered from 1-8 on the back and are pinned to the board with the numbers showing. The brown leaves introduce an element of chance so that a team member who answers a question incorrectly will not place their team in an irretrievable position.

You need a total of 16 questions from the Bible passage, 8 for each team.

Rules
A question is put to each group in turn and, if answered correctly, one of the team members chooses a leaf by calling out its number. The leaf is turned over and, if green, is pinned onto the stem. Brown leaves are discarded.

If an incorrect answer is given the question is offered to the other side.

Allow 10-15 minutes for the quiz.

PREPARATION

2 Chronicles 33:1-20

LESSON AIMS

To learn of God's mercy to repentant sinners.

The story of Manasseh is also found in 2 Kings 21:1-18. The Chronicles account differs in that, as well as showing all Manasseh's weakness, it also recounts Manasseh's capture by the Assyrians and deportation to Babylon, his repentance and his restoration as king in Jerusalem. The writer of Kings sees Manasseh as completely bad and almost single handedly responsible for the exile (2 Kings 21:10-15; 23:26-27). Some scholars think that the Chronicler recorded Manasseh's repentance in order to account for his long reign (length of reign being viewed as a blessing for obedience). However, length of reign is not noted as an indicator of divine blessing anywhere else in Chronicles - the usual measures of that were peace, prosperity, success at war, success with building and large families. It must be remembered that Chronicles was written post exile for those who had returned to Jerusalem.

33:1   55 years was a long reign, from 697-642 BC.

33:2-9   These verses contain a list of sins even worse, if possible, than those practised by his grandfather, Ahaz, including sorcery, occultism, and desecration of the temple (cf. Deuteronomy 18:9-14). Manasseh was outdoing the nations around in his level of wickedness (v.2,9).

33:11   Judah was subject to Assyria for much of Manasseh's reign, but there is no other record of Manasseh being deported to Babylon. In non-biblical references he is recorded as one amongst 21 other kings who had to supply building materials to Assyria, and as a vassal state supporting Assyria against Egypt.

13:12   Humiliation and distress brought about repentance.

33:14   The rebuilding of the outer wall was a sign of divine blessing (cf. 8:1-6; 11:5-12).

33:15-16   Whatever Manasseh did in the way of reform there was still more for Josiah to do when he came to the throne 2 years after Manasseh's death (see 2 Kings 23:4-12).

33:20   Manasseh was not accorded the privilege of burial in the tomb of the kings (cf. 21:20; 28:27).

QUESTIONS

1. Manasseh was a very wicked man, but repented of his sin. Look up 1 Timothy 1:15-17 to see what Paul said **he** was like prior to his conversion. What do these verses and the passage in Chronicles tell us about God's mercy?

2. God graciously heard Manasseh's prayer and forgave him, but Manasseh left a legacy for his people, i.e. exile. The Bible records others who, although forgiven, suffer the consequences of their sin (or leave a legacy of suffering for others). Can you think of any of them? What does this teach about the consequences of sin?

Consequences   Give each person a piece of paper and a pen and ask them a series of questions (see below). The answer to each question is written at the top of the paper, then folded over to hide the writing and passed to the person on their left, ready for the next question. At the end of the questions the papers are unfolded and the resulting scenarios read out to the group.

Introduce the activity by telling the group that they are writing an adventure story. Ask them to write down the following:

1. The name of the hero or heroine (could be real or fictional).

2. Where he or she went.

3. What did they plan to do when they got there?

4. Who or what did they meet?

5. What did they forget to take with them?

6. What happened as a result?

Link into the Bible passage by pointing out that the stories were about someone who suffered the consequences of his or her behaviour. Let's look at one of the worst kings in Judah's history and see the consequences of his behaviour.

Photocopy page 84 for each group member. The word is 'repentant'.

The letters which make up the answers to the 9 clues can be found in the grid below. Each group of 3 letters comes at the end of a word. Cross off the letters as you use them and write the answers in the bottom grid. When this is correctly completed the letters in the outlined column can be rearranged to complete the word missing from the sentence at the bottom of the page.

AH	AS	AS	AN	AY	BA	BY	DS	ED
EL	ER	FF	FT	GO	GS	HC	HE	HE
IN	KI	KO	LE	LON	MP	PR	RA	RAH
RIA	SY	TC	TE	TH	TW	VE	WI	ZE

1. How old was Manasseh when he became king?
2. What type of pole did Manasseh make?
3. Where did Manasseh build altars to the starry hosts? (4,6)
4. What 'w' did Manasseh practise?
5. The name of Manasseh's father.
6. Which country did God bring against Jerusalem?
7. Where was Manasseh taken when he was captured?
8. What 'p' did Manasseh do after he was captured?
9. What 't' did Manasseh sacrifice on the restored altar in God's temple?

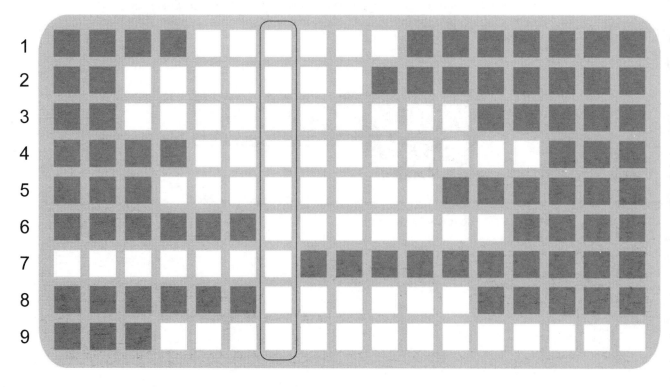

Manasseh learned that God will forgive a _ _ _ _ _ _ _ _ _ sinner.

PREPARATION

2 Chronicles
34:1 - 35:27

LESSON AIMS

To teach the importance of obeying God's word.

34:1-2 Josiah was 8 years old when he became king. His reign came after 57 years of religious rebellion, firstly under his grandfather Manasseh and then under his father Amon. The reformation he instituted, therefore, contrasts all the more with the religious environment into which he was born. But the accounts in Chronicles and Kings (2 Kings 22 - 23) suggest that perhaps Josiah was a Canute-like figure, trying to hold back the tide of religious apostasy unleashed upon Judah by the reign of Manasseh. The rot had gone too far. This may explain why, even though the reign of Josiah is approximately contemporary with the prophet Jeremiah, there is only one mention of the prophet in the Chronicles' account and that is at Josiah's death (2 Chronicles 35:25). By being obedient to God's word, Josiah was doing nothing more than was expected of him, but Jeremiah's ministry was to the nation of Judah and rebellion was still rife in the hearts of the people.

34:3-7 Eighth year .. twelfth ...eighteenth year. The main reason for the gradual introduction of the reform was that it was political as well as religious. In Josiah's eighth year Ashurbanipal, the last great king of Assyria, died. Failure to worship the Assyrian gods, and even more the removal of their symbols and altars from the Temple, would be regarded as a sign of rebellion. Josiah and his advisors evidently felt that they must act slowly to test the water.

34:8-9 Manasseh, Ephraim and the entire remnant of Israel is probably referring to those from the northern tribes who had settled in the south (11:16; 15:9), rather than to those left in the north.

34:15-19 Commentators suggest the book of the Law was either Deuteronomy, or a substantial part of it.

34:22 This verse is an extraordinary testimony to the accuracy of this record. Any story teller would surely have put the prophecy into the mouths of one of Josiah's great contemporary prophets, Jeremiah or Zephaniah.

34:29-32 The Covenant relationship between God and his people is re-established.

35:1-19 Josiah's Passover. The large numbers of animals were needed for the peace offerings during the Feast of Unleavened Bread and were mainly eaten by the worshippers.

35:11-13 It would seem that the actual Passover sacrifices and the later sacrifices of the week have, for the sake of brevity, been amalgamated.

35:18 The Passover had been overshadowed by the Feast of Tabernacles, celebrated as the New Year festival.

35:20 Carchemish was the place where the Egyptians and Assyrians joined together to oppose the Babylonians, who were the growing power.

35:21 Note that the king of Egypt says he is acting on God's commands. Josiah would have been wiser to have listened (cf. v.23-24)!

NB The significance of Josiah's obedience is that he patiently persevered even though at times he must have felt painfully alone. Apparently he was ignored by the prophet and opposed by the people. Even Huldah's message spoke only of the humble heart of the king, ignoring the whole subject of Josiah's reforms and concentrating on the rebellious heart of Judah. If the thought 'why bother?' ever crossed his mind, it was never allowed to distract him from his commitment to obeying God's word. Throughout the passage the impression given is that these were Josiah's reforms - 'he made all', 'he convened', 'he read'. The people concurred but were not convinced. Contrast this with the reforms in Hezekiah's time when the people were given 'one heart to obey the call to return to the Lord' (30:12). Obeying God's word can be difficult and even more so when we seem to be wasting our time. Josiah's lesson is of tremendous importance for us and the group.

1. Josiah did what was right, even when there was no obvious support. What was his motivation? What changed his life?

2. The people went along with Josiah's reforms as long as he was alive (34:33), but then reverted back to their idolatry after his death. What does this teach us about our own faith and responsibility? Do we only do things out of respect for our parent's faith?

See map on page 69.

Keeping Going   Divide the group into teams. Place one bucket for each team at one end of the room. The teams start at the other end of the room and must take it in turns to bat a balloon down to the room and into the bucket using only a rolled up tube of newspaper. Once the balloon is in the bucket the player picks it up and runs back to his team, handing the paper tube and balloon to the next player. The first team to complete the task wins. You need some extra balloons in case any burst.

Link in to the Bible study by pointing out the difficulty of the task and the need to persevere in order to complete it successfully. Let's see how well King Josiah remained obedient to God's word, even when it was difficult to do so.

This activity can be done in teams or as individuals. Photocopy page 88 for each group/member. The statements and numbers can be cut out prior to the activity to make it easier to match them up. The 2 unanswerable questions are, 'How many Levites celebrated the Passsover?' and, 'How old was Josiah when they found the Book of the Law?' The 2 unused numbers are 24 and 300.

Match up the following statements and answers (numbers). To see what you have remembered, try and do it without using your Bibles. Two wrong statements and answers have been included in the list.

How old was Josiah when he became king?	1
How many years did Josiah reign?	7
How old was Josiah when he began to destroy the shrines to foreign gods?	8
How many Levites celebrated the Passover?	14
How old was Josiah when he started repairs to the temple?	16
How many cattle did Josiah provide for the Passover?	20
In which month was the Passover lamb killed?	24
How old was Josiah when he began to seek God?	26
How many sheep and goats did Josiah provide for the Passover?	31
How old was Josiah when they found the Book of the Law?	300
How many days did the Feast of Unleavened Bread last?	3,000
On what day of the month was the Passover lamb killed?	30,000

PREPARATION

2 Chronicles 36:1-23,
Jeremiah 39:1-10

LESSON AIMS

To see the outcome
of persistent
disobedience.

2 Chronicles

36:1   With the death of Josiah at Pharaoh's hand, Judah once more came under Egyptian domination, ending a brief 20 year period of independence under Josiah.

Jehoahaz was the fourth son of Josiah. He reigned for 3 months before being deposed by the king of Egypt (v.2-3).

36:3   The tribute exacted would have been taken probably from the Temple.

36:4   Jehoahaz was taken into captivity in Egypt. Eliakim was the second son of Josiah. Each conqueror changed the name of the king he put into power as it implied his authority over him.

36:5   Jehoiakim persecuted the prophets and is the object of a scathing attack by Jeremiah (Jeremiah 25:1-11). After the Egyptians had been defeated at Carchemish in 605 BC Jehoiakim transferred allegiance to Nebuchadnezzar of Babylon. When he later rebelled and again allied himself with Egypt, Nebuchadnezzar sent an army against him. Jehoiakim may not have been taken into captivity (cf. 2 Kings 24:1,6), but he was subject to Babylon until the end of his reign.

36:9   Jehoiachin was the son of Jehoiakim and grandson of Josiah. He reigned for only 3 months before being deposed by the king of Babylon.

36:11   Zedekiah was the third son of Josiah.

36:12-13 Zedekiah was proud and he refused to listen to God's message through Jeremiah. He took an oath of allegiance to Nebuchadnezzar, swearing on God's name, which he later broke, thus bringing disgrace on the House of David. Nebuchadnezzar had made the mistake of deporting the majority of the leading statesmen of Judah with Jehoiachin 10 years earlier (2 Kings 24:15-16). Those left were men of less maturity and wisdom, who advised Zedekiah wrongly (cf. Jeremiah 38:1-5). Zedekiah was given a clear message through Jeremiah, but failed to act on it (Jeremiah 38:14-27).

36:20-21 See Jeremiah 25:1-11.

36:22-23 See Jeremiah 29:10-14. These verses are identical to Ezra 1:1-3.

Jeremiah

39:1-2   The siege of Jerusalem lasted for 18 months, during which time the city suffered all the horrors of famine.

39:3-10 These verses give a graphic picture of the fall and sacking of Jerusalem and capture of Zedekiah.

QUESTIONS

1. Summarise all the blessings God had given his people under Solomon's rule (1 Kings 4:20-25; 8:55-66; 10:23-25). Then compare them with Judah at the end of Zedekiah's reign. What had gone wrong?

2. What does this passage teach about persistent disobedience of God? Does there ever come a time when it is too late to repent? Is there anything in the passage to give hope for the future?

Keeping the Rules   Line up chairs in several rows, one chair for each group member. Explain that you will be looking at the importance of rules. Read out a list of statements containing commonly broken rules one at a time (see below). Each time you read out a statement the group members must move as directed. Ensure that the group understand the following rules before starting the game:

1. You must respond truthfully.

2. If directed to move to a seat already occupied, sit on that person's lap.

3. If you reach the end of a row and still have moves to make, run to the other end of the row and continue.

4. If you reach the front and still have moves to make, run to the back and continue and vice versa.

Statements
1. If you have ever crossed the road when the green man is red, move 1 seat to your right.

2. If you have ever cheated at sport, move 3 seats back.

3. If you have ever cheated during one of our games, move 2 seats to your right.

4. If you have ever truanted from school, move 2 seats back and 1 to your right.

5. If you have ever ridden a bike on the road at night without lights, move 3 seats forward.

6. If you have ever copied someone else's homework, move 2 seats right and 2 seats forward.

7. If you have ever disobeyed your parents, move 3 seats left and 4 seats back.

8. If you have ever broken a school rule, move 2 seats forward and 4 seats left.

9. If you have not moved from your seat during the game you have broken the first rule, so move 3 seats back and 4 seats right.

By this time there should be chaos.

Link in to the Bible study by pointing out that the reason they ended up in such a mess was because they had broken different rules. Let's see what happened as a result of King Zedekiah's disobedience.

This activity is a game designed to revise the whole of the series on the Kings. The game should be played in groups of 5-6. For each group photocopy page 90 at A3 size and glue onto card to make a board. Photocopy pages 91, 92 and 93 on card for each group and cut up to make a pack of question cards. Other requirements and the instructions for playing the game are written on page 90.

43	44 **Q**	45	46 **Q**	47	48 Judah is under Egyptian domination. Go back to square 32	49 **Exile in Babylon**
42 **Q**	41	40 Josiah is made king. Go forward 1 square	39 Manasseh repents. Go forward 2 squares.	38	37 **Q**	36
29 **Q**	30	31 Jerusalem is under siege. Go back 1 square	32	33 **Q**	34	35 Manasseh is made king. Go back 3 squares.
28	27 Hezekiah is made king. Go forward 3 squares.	26 Israel is taken into captivity. Miss 1 turn.	25	24 **Q**	23	22 Josiah is made king. Go forward 3 squares.
15	16 **Q**	17	18 Athaliah kills all the royal family. Go back to the time of Samuel.	19	20 **Q**	21
14 Jehoshaphat strengthens Judah. Go forward 1 square	13	12 **Q**	11	10 **Q**	9	8 The kingdom is divided. Miss 1 turn.
1 **The Time of Samuel**	2	3 The Israelites ask for a king. Go back 1 square.	4	5 **Q**	6	7 David becomes king. Go forward 2 squares.

Required

Counters for each player.
1 dice
1 pack of Question cards (shuffled).

Instructions

1. Throw the dice to decide who starts - the person who throws the highest number.

2. The play then moves in a clockwise direction.

3. Each player throws the dice and moves the number thrown. If he/she lands on a square with instructions written on it, these instructions must be obeyed. If he/she lands on a square with **Q** written on it, one of the other players takes the top question card and reads out the question.

If the player answers correctly he/she moves forward 1 square.

For an incorrect answer the player moves backwards 1 square.

4. The first player to reach square 49, **'Exile in Babylon'**, wins.

NB for the teacher

This game is for revision of the Kings series. If an incorrect answer is given, see if any other player knows the answer. (A correct answer from another player does not result in that player's counter moving forward.)

Q Who was the first human king of Israel?

A Saul

Q Who was the first king of Judah following the division of the kingdom?

A Rehoboam

Q Who was the first king of Israel following the division of the kingdom?

A Jeroboam

Q How many of the 12 tribes were included in the kingdom of Israel?

A 10

Q How many of the 12 tribes were included in the kingdom of Judah?

A 2

Q Who did Ahab marry?

A Jezebel

Q Whose vineyard did Ahab covet?

A Naboth's

Q Which prophet confronted Ahab with his sin?

A Elijah

Q Which king of Judah made an alliance with king Ahab?

A Jehoshaphat

Q Where was Joash hidden for the first 6 years of his life?

A In the temple.

Q Who was the major influence on Joash while he was growing up?

A Jehoiada, the priest

Q What was restored in the time of Joash?

A The temple

Q What did Joash order done to Zechariah?

A He was stoned to death.

Q Which king besieged Jerusalem in the time of Hezekiah?

A Sennacherib, king of Assyria

Q Who was Hezekiah's son?

A Manasseh

Q What was rebuilt during the time of Manasseh?

A The outer wall of Jerusalem.

Q To which king was Hezekiah compared?

A David

Q Which prophet told Hezekiah that God would deliver Jerusalem from the enemy?

A Isaiah

Q What did Manasseh build in the temple?

A Altars to worship all the starry hosts.

Q How old was Josiah when he became king?

A 8

Q Which symbol dating from Israel's past did Hezekiah destroy?

A The bronze snake.

Q To whom did Hezekiah show all his treasures?

A Messengers from the king of Babylon.

Q Where was Manasseh taken as a prisoner?

A To Babylon.

Q What was found in the temple storehouse in the time of Josiah?

A The Book of the Law.

Q Which feast was celebrated in the time of Josiah in a way not seen since the time of Samuel? **A** The Passover	**Q** Which king was Josiah fighting against when he was killed? **A** Neco, king of Egypt
Q Why did God allow the Babylonians to capture Jerusalem and destroy the temple? **A** Because his people had turned to follow other gods.	**Q** What was the name of the last king of Judah? **A** Zedekiah
Q What does 2 Chronicles 7:14 say? **A** If my people, who are called by my name, will humble themselves and pray and seek my face and turn from their wicked ways, then will I hear from heaven and will forgive their sin and will heal their land.	**Q** Give the Bible reference for – If my people, who are called by my name, will humble themselves and pray and seek my face and turn from their wicked ways, then will I hear from heaven and will forgive their sin and will heal their land. **A** 2 Chronicles 7:14
Q Which king besieged Jerusalem and took the people captive? **A** Nebuchadnezzar	
Q What does 2 Chronicles 7:14 say? **A** If my people, who are called by my name, will humble themselves and pray and seek my face and turn from their wicked ways, then will I hear from heaven and will forgive their sin and will heal their land.	
Q Give the Bible reference for – If my people, who are called by my name, will humble themselves and pray and seek my face and turn from their wicked ways, then will I hear from heaven and will forgive their sin and will heal their land. **A** 2 Chronicles 7:14	

Bible Timeline

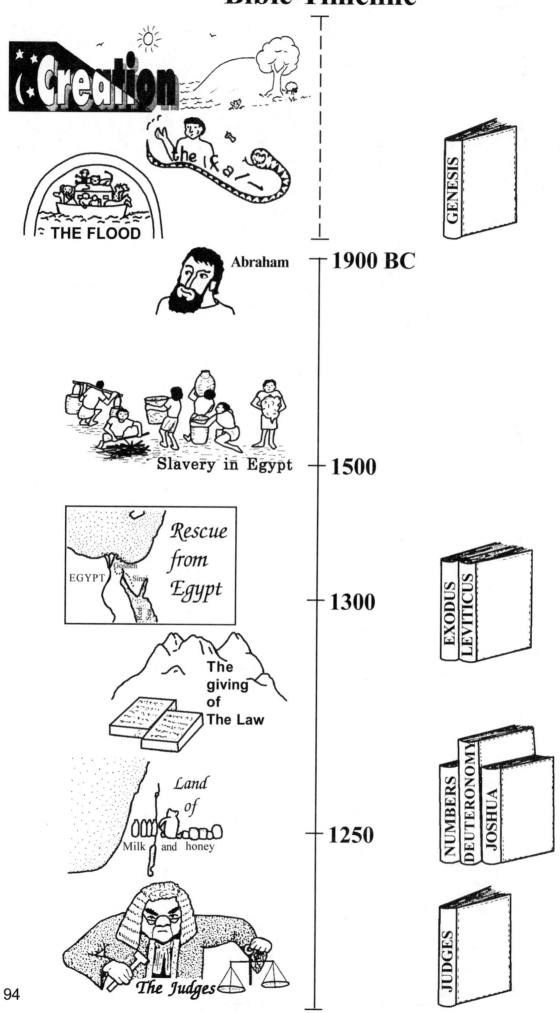

Creation

the fall

THE FLOOD

GENESIS

1900 BC

Abraham

Slavery in Egypt

1500

Rescue from Egypt

EGYPT Goshen Sinai Red Sea

EXODUS LEVITICUS

1300

The giving of The Law

Land of Milk and honey

NUMBERS DEUTERONOMY JOSHUA

1250

The Judges

JUDGES

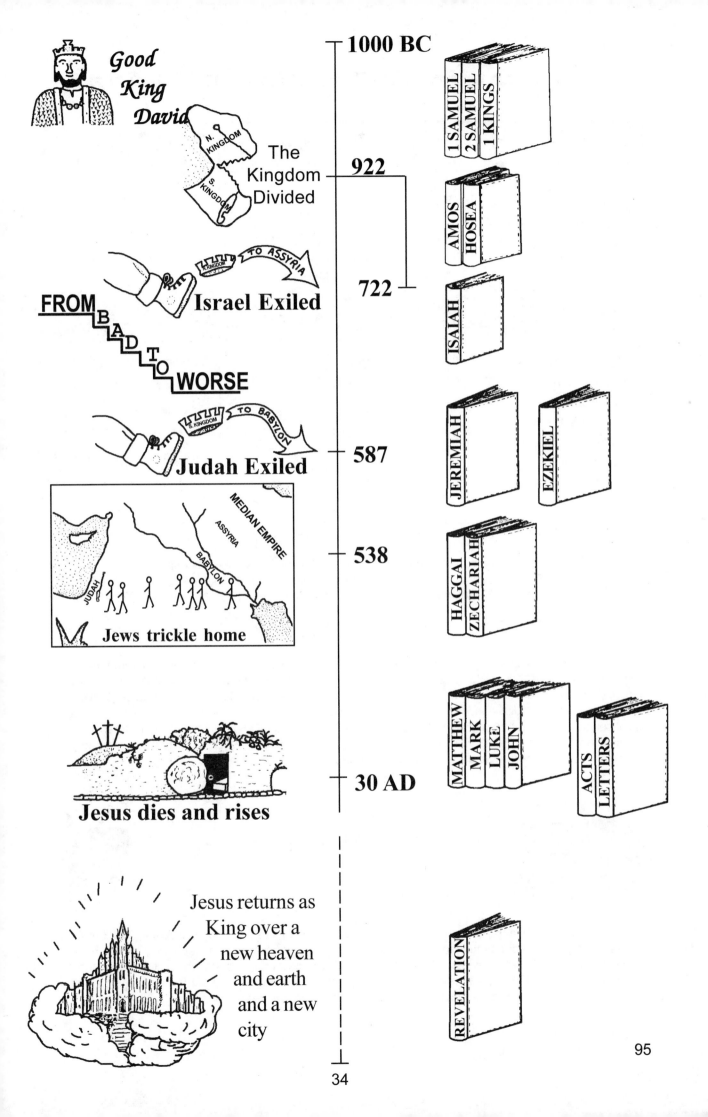

Good King David

The Kingdom Divided

N. KINGDOM

S. KINGDOM

1000 BC

922

1 SAMUEL 2 SAMUEL 1 KINGS

N.KINGDOM TO ASSYRIA

Israel Exiled

FROM BAD TO WORSE

722

AMOS HOSEA

ISAIAH

S. KINGDOM TO BABYLON

Judah Exiled

587

JEREMIAH EZEKIEL

MEDIAN EMPIRE

ASSYRIA

BABYLON

JUDAH

Jews trickle home

538

HAGGAI ZECHARIAH

Jesus dies and rises

30 AD

MATTHEW MARK LUKE JOHN ACTS LETTERS

Jesus returns as King over a new heaven and earth and a new city

REVELATION

95

34

Syllabus for On The Way for 11-14s

Book 1 (28 weeks)	Book 3 (28 weeks)	Book 5 (26 weeks)
Abraham (7) Jacob (7) The Messiah (Christmas) (2) Jesus said, 'I am …' (7) Ruth (5)	Joseph (7) People in Prayer (7) The Saviour of the World (Christmas)(3) Is God Fair? (Predestination) (2) Learning from a Sermon (3) The Sermon on the Mount (6)	Bible Overview (26)
Book 2 (25 weeks)	**Book 4 (25 weeks)**	**Book 6 (27 weeks)**
Rescue (Easter) (3) Paul (Acts 9-16) (7) Philippians (5) Paul (Acts 17-18) (3) 1 Thessalonians (6) Suffering (1)	Psalms (Easter) (2) Paul's Latter Ministry (7) Colossians (5) Choose Life (Hell & Judgment) (2) The Kings (9)	A Selection of Psalms (5) The Normal Christian Life (7) Revelation (9) Homosexuality (1) The Dark Days of the Judges (5)

The books can be used in any order. The number in brackets indicates the number of lessons in a series.

For more information about *On the Way for 11-14s* please contact:
Christian Focus Publications, Fearn, Tain, Ross-shire, IV20 1TW / Tel: +44 (0) 1862 871 011 or
TnT Ministries, 29 Buxton Gardens, Acton, London, W3 9LE / Tel: +44 (0) 20 8992 0450

Christian Focus Publications publishes books for adults and children under its three main imprints: Christian Focus; Mentor and Christian Heritage. Our books reflect that God's word is reliable and Jesus is the way to know him, and live forever with him. Our children's publication list includes a Sunday school curriculum that covers pre-school to early teens; puzzle and activity books. We also publish personal and family devotional titles, biographies and inspirational stories that children will love. If you are looking for quality Bible teaching for children then we have an excellent range of Bible story and age specific theological books. From pre-school to teenage fiction, we have it covered! ***Find us at our web page: www.christianfocus.com***

TnT Ministries

TnT Ministries (which stands for Teaching and Training Ministries) was launched in February 1993 by Christians from a broad variety of denominational backgrounds who were concerned that teaching the Bible to children be taken seriously. The leaders were in charge of the Sunday School of 50 teachers at St Helen's Bishopsgate, an evangelical church in the City of London, for 13 years, during which time a range of Biblical teaching materials was developed. TnT Ministries also runs training days for Sunday School teachers.